GENERATION
EARN

GENERATION EARN

The Young Professional's Guide to

SPENDING, INVESTING,
and GIVING BACK

KIMBERLY PALMER

TEN SPEED PRESS
Berkeley

Library of Congress Cataloging-in-Publication Data

Palmer, Kimberly.
 Generation earn : the young professional's guide to spending, investing, and
giving back / by Kimberly Palmer. — 1st ed.
  p. cm.
 Includes bibliographical references and index.
 Summary: "Personal finance columnist Kimberly Palmer gives up-and-coming
young professionals, who are tired of being referred to as 'generation debt,' smart
advice that bolsters their financial goals for themselves, their budding families,
and the global community"—Provided by publisher.
 1. Professional employees—Finance, Personal. 2. Young adults—Finance, Personal. 3. Finance, Personal. I. Title.
 HG179.P1886 2010
 332.024—dc22
 2010008797

ISBN 978-1-58008-236-5

Printed in the United States of America

Front cover photograph copyright © Lawrence Manning/Corbis

Design by Betsy Stromberg

10 9 8 7 6 5 4 3 2 1

First Edition

For Sujay and Kareena

Contents

Part 1 BUILDING YOUR LIFE

Part 2 CREATING A HOME

Part 3 CHANGING THE WORLD

Acknowledgments

First, I give my thanks to everyone quoted in this book who shared their stories and experiences so openly with me. By walking me through your intimate decision-making processes, lessons learned, and concerns, you helped turn otherwise-dry personal finance topics into something much more interesting, and you made the process of writing this book much more enjoyable for me.

My agent, Melissa Sarver, provided the energy, enthusiasm, feedback, and support that made this book possible. My editor at Ten Speed Press, Lisa Westmoreland, also gave invaluable guidance. Thanks also to my publicist, Kara Van de Water.

I would also like to thank the editors and mentors who have helped me since I first started in journalism, including Jim Bock, Nik Deogun, Peggy Engel, Peggy Hackman, Anne Laurent, Jim Pethokoukis, and Tom Shoop. I am also so appreciative of the support of my colleagues at *US News & World Report*, especially Emily Brandon, Kim Castro, Katy Marquardt, Tim Smart, and Liz Wolgemuth. Many thanks to my friends and family members who provided their expertise and feedback on early drafts, especially Tom Biggins, Alison Comfort, Nilay Davé, Ned Friend, Catherine Hirschman, Pegg Hoffman, Claire Moodie, Hayley Rohn-Davé, and Karen Rutzick.

My parents, Chris Palmer and Gail Shearer, and my sisters, Christina and Jennifer Palmer, gave me constant support, both personal and professional, as I worked on this book and throughout my entire life, for which I am infinitely grateful.

By some fluke of timing, my baby and this book shared the same due date. Meeting both deadlines was only possible with the constant and endless support of my husband, Sujay Davé. Not only did he listen and give me feedback as I read much of the book out loud to him during car trips but he also made the entire process of getting ready for a baby and writing a book as fun and relaxing as it could possibly be.

Introduction: Meet the New Young Professional

As the twenty-first century began, journalists and financial advisers began throwing around a new term to describe the current group of young people: Generation Debt. This term evoked slackers who lacked their grandparents' sense of financial responsibility—instead of saving for a rainy day, they wasted their money on lattes, iPods, and takeout. These people were made to seem as though they lived off credit cards, student loans, and whatever help their parents could send their way.

This mythical tribe soon had its own spokespeople and leaders. Reporters found scores of young professionals caught up in spiraling credit card debt willing to dish about the forces that had created their mess. In response, popular books advocated eating ramen and reusing popcorn bags to get free refills at the movies.[1] Before long, a *Village Voice* column and two books, one with a subtitle that called our era a "terrible time to be young," were named after the alleged phenomenon.[2] The financial crisis of 2008 and 2009 generated even more extreme stories of woe: the *Minneapolis Star Tribune* profiled a twenty-five-year-old with $94,000 in student loan debt who was resigned, permanently it seemed, to living in her in-laws' basement.[3] NBC's *Today Show* featured a handful of twenty-somethings with various degrees of credit card, student loan, and car loan debt. "I don't even go get a Starbucks," bemoaned one. "When I go to the gas station I don't get a drink. I don't—nothing. I can't afford it."[4]

Pundits used these kinds of examples in order to justify an increasingly condescending attitude about our financial aptitude. On the Fox Business Network, Beth Kobliner, author of the best-seller *Get a Financial Life*, said that even Ivy League college students graduate without understanding how to pay for everyday expenses. She recalled one student who asked her how to take out a loan to rent an apartment, and she had to explain that people use income, not loans, to pay their rent. "Basic, basic concepts they just don't know about money," she said.[5]

The term *generation debt* stuck because there is some truth to it. Two out of three college students now take out student loans, compared to less than half in 1993.[6] By the time the typical graduate walks across the stage to pick up his diploma, he owes $22,700.[7] Average credit card debt among twenty-five- to thirty-four-year-olds has climbed 50 percent since 1989, to over $4,000 per person.[8]

But most of us are not letting our debts define us. While student loan burdens are heavier than they were in generations past, more of us have college and advanced degrees that give us greater earning power. The number of people enrolled in graduate programs has increased over 70 percent since 1976, making Generations X and Y the most highly educated group of Americans to date.[9] Meanwhile, our incomes have largely been underestimated; studies by the Federal Reserve Bank of Minneapolis show that, with adjustments for inflation and benefits, the median compensation rate has gone up 28 percent since 1975.[10]

As for credit cards, only one in three college students carries one at all.[11] The average amount owed is just $495. Among twenty-five- to thirty-four-year-olds, more than half pay off their entire balance each month.[12] And, when asked how we feel about our economic standing, most of us say we feel pretty good. In a 2009 Pew survey, six in ten respondents under the age of forty said their standard of living is much or somewhat better than that of their parents at the same age, while just 15 percent said it is worse.[13] This is true even though many of us experienced two recessions before reaching mid-career, first when the tech bubble burst in 2001 and then when the subprime mortgage crisis led to housing market collapses and bank failures in 2008 and 2009.

However, all these facts and figures don't quite capture the zeitgeist of our generation. Few would mistake us for self-satisfied Alex P. Keaton types, reaping the bounties of capitalism. The popping of the tech bubble and the subprime mortgage crisis underscored the importance of sacrifice and hard work and made it clear how hard it can be to get ahead. Nor are we purely do-gooders—college kids canvassing for their political idols. We are something in between. We want to own nice homes, feel financially successful, support our families, one day send our kids to college, and change the world at the same time.

Although we may now have some money to invest, our goals involve far more than just becoming rich. The financial crisis of 2008 dovetailed with a growing interest in sustainability, simplicity, and even frugality. Instead of living exclusively for our own pleasures, we have embraced a new level of social consciousness. We care about the environment, our cities, and social justice. Many of us also want kids, and, thanks in part to loud warnings about the decline of fertility with age, we aren't putting that off forever, either.

As the "Alpha Consumer" blogger and columnist for *US News & World Report*, I frequently receive questions from readers about navigating this terrain: What should I be doing with my savings? Where should I invest my money? Can I afford to buy a house, or should I keep renting? Does it make sense to share a mortgage with my boyfriend? Can I afford a baby? How can I support the causes I believe in? As a young professional myself, I have many of the same concerns.

This book explores those questions and gives you tools to help you make the best decisions for your situation. It explains how to improve your bank account as well as how to get closer to reaching your bigger financial ambitions, from living debt free to saving for a child's future college education. It looks at how to manage money in relationships, both before and during marriage. It asks when it makes sense to accept financial aid from parents, and how to handle requests for assistance from other family members. It will help you decide whether you're ready to buy a house, have a baby, or take a break from your career. It also explains how to make an impact on the world with your money and resources, whether that means starting a nonprofit or spending and investing in a way that supports your values.

Along the way, we'll meet twenty-, thirty-, and forty-somethings who have faced those challenges themselves. Before moving in together, Chicago couple Pasha Carroll and Matthew Krise wondered how they should combine, or not combine, their bank accounts. They give partial credit for the success of their relationship to their solution—to keep almost everything separate—although many couples find combining everything equally satisfying. Kate and Thomas Deriso show us why cooking and even growing some of their own food in northern Virginia isn't a sacrifice but a way to live more richly. Keith and Katy Hewson decided that the best way to start out married life was to live with Katy's parents in their Houston townhouse. While the older couple covered the mortgage payments, Keith and Katy pulled their weight by handling most of the monthly bills, which meant each couple saved thousands of dollars. Lindsay Hyde, a twenty-eight-year-old from southern Florida, turned her passion for mentoring young girls into a nonprofit that now operates in three cities.

Each of their paths began with questions: How should we manage our money together? Is there a way to afford the lifestyle we want? How can I feel like I'm making an impact without sacrificing my own financial security? My husband and I also grappled with these issues as we prepared for the birth of our first child while I wrote this book. In the process, we weighed the pros and cons of moving into a bigger place, taking out life insurance, and saving for our daughter's future college education versus putting money away for our own retirements.

Our generation doesn't need to define itself by debt and financial struggle, but we do face new challenges and trade-offs. I hope this book helps you to navigate them.

Part 1

BUILDING YOUR LIFE

1

THE JOY OF SPENDING

We can finally afford some of the luxuries that were out of reach when we were struggling college students and entry-level employees. But, in addition to reaping some of the rewards of our hard work, we also need to prioritize financial security. Because the cost of living has gone up while job security has gone down, getting ahead requires saving a higher percentage of our incomes than any previous generation has before.

In this chapter, you'll learn how to do the following:

1. Define your financial goals, even the ones that cost as much as a Manhattan townhouse

2. Create a spending plan that makes sense for your lifestyle

3. Win the consumer wars that lead to overspending

DISNEY WORLD OR SOY LATTES?

I met Kimberly Wilson, a yoga teacher, author, and entrepreneur, on an early spring day in Washington, DC, at a coffee shop in Dupont Circle to find out how she had turned so many of her goals into reality. I'd been a longtime reader of her blog, "Tranquility du Jour," which discusses how to apply the lessons of yoga to everyday life. In addition to teaching yoga and designing her own line of ecofriendly clothing, she runs a foundation to help young women and was in the midst of opening a new yoga studio down the street when we spoke.

"I'm a saver," she told me as we sat down. "But I also think self-care is so important. Massages, candles . . . simple indulgences can be a small amount of money but contribute to overall happiness." She mostly wears her own designs, supplemented with items from Target and other discount stores; she picked up her dangly earrings for $2.99 at H&M. (Not that she sacrifices fashion—her long black dress and oversized sunglasses looked like something celebrity stylist Rachel Zoe would put together.)

Instead of buying clothes, Kimberly, who's in her mid-thirties, puts her money toward the big and little things that are important to her. She recently borrowed $500,000, largely through a bank loan, to build the new studio. She's saving to buy a cabin in West Virginia where she, her boyfriend, and pug dog can escape for weekend getaways. Over the previous three days, she had made career-investment purchases to help inspire her own designs (a $132 Victoria's Secret dress and a $19 Target dress). She had also bought fire logs for cozy evenings at home as well as soy lattes and cupcakes to inject some treats into her daily routine.

Give yourself a financial refresher course. Here are some of the top resources for creating a personal tutorial:

- **mymoney.gov:** Run by the federal government, this site collects information from multiple federal agencies and walks visitors through banking, home ownership, and retirement planning basics.
- **americasaves.org:** Through stories, tips, and online tools, this website teaches people how to save more money.
- **smartaboutmoney.org:** This site, run by the National Endowment for Financial Education, provides detailed information on insurance, paying for college, buying a home, and dozens of other scenarios.

Kimberly's choices might look lopsided to someone else (half a million dollars for her business and $3 for earrings?), but they reflect her priorities. Identifying those priorities isn't always easy, especially when they stray from the popular goals of buying a house or starting a baby fund. To help determine their priorities, Kimberly often urges people to ask themselves what they would do if they weren't limited by time or money.

You can also start with the idea of receiving $1,000. When I asked my Alpha Consumer blog readers what they would do with such a windfall, their answers included the following:

- Take the kids to Disney World

- Donate to charity

- Invest in the stock market

- Put it into a high-yield savings account for a future down payment

- Pay off bills and loans

- Buy a bike

- Build a greenhouse

- Buy a new laptop

- Buy luxury groceries like almond butter and high-quality tea

- Go on a Caribbean escape, leaving the serious books and to-do list at home

- Help enable wife to work part-time while she pursues hobby of textile design and husband to stay in the low-paying job that he loves

In addition to the sometime-before-I-die goals, shorter-term ones might include paying off high-interest student loan debt, increasing savings, or staying at a five-star hotel.

☑ Quick Tip: Budgeting by the Year

Research suggests that creating an annual budget instead of a monthly one works best, largely because we feel less confident in our annual estimates, so tend to add more cushioning for unexpected expenses. In one study, college students underestimated their monthly expenses by 40 percent while overestimating their annual expenses by 3 percent.[1]

In order to achieve those goals, you will need to build a spending plan that makes them possible. For most people, about two-thirds of their spending goes toward the essentials: food, housing, and transportation.[2] It's best for those staples to use up no more than half of a person's take-home pay, but it can be hard to find any money left over after paying for that increasingly pricey trifecta.

That means the average young professional, a thirty-year-old business consultant in Austin, Texas—let's call him Kenneth—with a salary of, say, $80,000 a year, will take home, after paying taxes and adding to his retirement account, about $48,000. To spend only half of that on housing, food, and transportation, he'd need to spend roughly $15,000 on rent (unless he's built up savings, there's no room for a mortgage), $6,000 on food (about $115 a week, including at-home meals as well as lunches and dinners out), and $3,000 on transportation (almost $12 a day, which includes any car-related expenses, such as purchasing one). For Kenneth, following those guidelines isn't easy, especially since he likes to go out to bars with his friends on the weekends and take his girlfriend, Danielle, to nice restaurants. But he makes it happen; his apartment is near a bus stop that allows for an easy commute to work and he eats simple meals at home during the week (he's usually too busy to go out anyway), so he can save his cash for weekend splurges.

After those basics, the next most pressing demand on young professionals' salaries is debt payments. Most of us have monthly student loan bills to pay. Kenneth graduated with $30,000 in debt, a modest sum compared to some of his peers. He pays around $200 a month toward it.

☑ Quick Tip: Track That Money

Spending plans for after-tax income should include these six components:
1. The basics: food, housing, and transportation
2. Debt payments
3. Savings
4. Professional expenses
5. Household expenses
6. Entertainment

The third priority is savings. Ideally, we should save about one-quarter of our pre-tax salaries (this includes retirement contributions). This is an ambitious goal, and close to impossible for those of us still shelling out two-thirds or more of our salaries for basic living costs. It might take several years of saving 5 to 10 percent before we reach this level, and there are likely to be periods—shortly after having children, for example—when savings drop significantly. To put it in perspective, the average American household saves less than 5 percent of its income.[3] But the goal should be to bank one out of every four dollars we bring home, in order to create an emergency cushion of at least three months' worth of living expenses as well as to save money for those big goals.

☑ Quick Tip: Lease or Buy?

While traditional wisdom says that buying a car is a better financial decision than leasing one, since with a lease you build no equity over time and are left with nothing once it's up, there are some circumstances in which leasing is the better choice. The main one is when your life plans are up in the air. If you might move overseas within a few years, take a job across the country, or suddenly expand your family, then leasing a car for the interim could end up being cheaper than buying one. In addition, manufacturers and dealers sometimes subsidize leases to such an extent that leasing turns out to be cheaper than buying. Visit the car site edmunds.com for a calculator that will help you decide if leasing is the better choice for you.

For Kenneth, that means saving a total of $20,000 each year. Part of that—10 percent of his salary, or $8,000—will go directly into the tax-protected 401(k) account offered by his consulting job. Of the remaining $12,000, half goes into his emergency savings account, which will cover his expenses if he gets laid off or suddenly needs to loan money to his sister, a struggling graphic designer in Portland, Oregon. The rest will go toward funding his goals, which include a trip to Ecuador with Danielle and, later, a condo.

The fourth priority is professional expenses—new outfits, dry cleaning, networking lunches. These are the investments that advance careers. The fifth and related category encompasses household expenses, which include items that enable better relaxation at night and better performance during the day. That could mean cable television, kitchenware, and grooming supplies. (No one wants unkempt employees.) Also included here are items such as maid services, delivery fees, and dog walking, which free up more energy and time for work.

The final priority is entertainment—we need to enjoy ourselves, whether it's through fancy dinners out, movies, travel, or weekend getaways. But it's also the area that gets squeezed first when the other priorities aren't met.

☑ Quick Tip: Savvy Traveling

Before making hotel reservations, check out your options for renting an apartment, especially if you're visiting an expensive country such as Italy or England. Websites often connect visitors with locals who rent out their centrally located apartments for a fraction of the price of a hotel. As an added bonus, having a kitchen means you can make your own breakfast, lunch, and sometimes dinner, which you might welcome after a few days of expensive, rich food. (Plus, you get the fun experience of shopping at a local grocery store.)

If you're going to be staying in more traditional accommodations, be sure to do your homework first through comparison websites such as tripadvisor.com to make sure you're getting the best deal. Previous visitors often post candid reviews and photos. Once you've selected your spot, you might want to consider calling the hotel to ask if they can give you a better deal or if breakfast can be included in the room rate, especially if it's off season.

Let's go back to those goals. Kenneth wants to travel and save for a condo. He'll have $6,000 in the bank dedicated to those purposes after year one on his new plan. Although he could never have accomplished that in his early twenties, when he was still in grad school and, later, a junior analyst, now he has a fuller cash cushion. His savings make it possible for him and Danielle to go to Ecuador together.

They do make the trip, and as they tour the Galapagos Islands, he proposes to her. This propels them into a new and more complicated stage of financial management, which will eventually cause Kenneth to reexamine his financial priorities, adjust his spending style, and, after they start a family, reinvent his career.

☑ Quick Tip: Money to Go

Instead of converting a handful of bills to local currency before you get on the plane, consider sticking with plastic instead. By waiting until you arrive to withdraw money from an ATM, you can avoid some of the bank transaction fees. Even better, limit your use of cash and rely primarily on credit cards, which typically charge lower fees than ATMs. Credit cards vary widely in their fee structure, though, so be sure to ask your card company for its policy ahead of time and use the card with the lowest fee. Using credit cards also limits your risk of fraud and theft, and you can review all the charges on your statement once you return home. Just be sure to let your bank know about your travel plans before you take off, however, since if they see the charges made in another country they might think your card has been stolen and freeze your account before they can track you down. (Traveler's checks used to be the best way to bring money with you across borders, but the ease of using plastic and conducting electronic transactions has rendered them almost obsolete.)

If saving enough to fund your goals seems impossible—say you want to spend three months visiting every medieval church in Europe, or become the owner of a five-bedroom home in San Francisco—then you might need to make some adjustments to your goals. Instead of sampling the cuisine in Tuscany, how about starting with a cooking class at Sur La Table? If you want to adopt two dogs but are still struggling to pay your rent, how about volunteering at a rescue shelter once a week? Perhaps a used Honda Accord can temporarily substitute for a new Volkswagen Touareg.

Here's an overview of how much to aim to spend in each category (all percentages are based on after-tax income, with the exception of savings, which includes pre-tax retirement fund contributions):

1. The basics—food, housing, and transportation: 50 percent

2. Debt payments: Less than 5 percent

3. Savings: 25 percent

4. Professional expenses: Less than 5 percent

5. Household expenses: Less than 5 percent

6. Entertainment: 5 percent

These categories add up to less than 100 percent in order to allow for some wiggle room. You can personalize your plan to fit your own needs, such as child-care costs, large student loan payments, or a scuba-diving hobby.

☑ Quick Tip: In Praise of Screw Caps

Buy screw-top wine. There's a heated debate raging in the world of oenophiles over whether screw tops or corks are better, but screw caps generally keep wine fresher and eliminate the risk of wine becoming "corked," or going bad while the cork is in place, which happens in around 1 to 10 percent of corked bottles. Bottles with screw caps are also generally cheaper than their cork-topped counterparts. Corks are often a good choice for bottles that will age in cellars for long periods of time, but if you'll be drinking that wine soon after purchasing, you might as well go for a screw cap. So unless you're talking about an expensive bottle of Bordeaux that's aging in your wine cellar, the twist-off top works just as well. It also takes less time to open, which means you'll be drinking it sooner.

THE TYRANNY—AND BEAUTY—OF LIST MAKING

Now it's time to get down to the nitty-gritty with a temporary foray into obsessive-compulsiveness. The first time I began keeping a spending diary, I was skeptical. I thought I already knew my weak spots—bottles of wine, taxis, and sushi.

I was wrong. The first day, I spent $136 on groceries and $60 on a new pillow. Monday through Thursday, I bought three cappuccinos, subway rides, and one lunch—pretty standard. But then, on Friday and Saturday, my husband and I spent $54 on a casual dinner and then $80 on a dinner out with friends. So we spent $134 in restaurants in one weekend without even thinking about it. Shortly after, we started eating out only one night a week, and I felt better about my weekday spending.

We also used the concept of a spending diary when we were trying to decide whether or not to buy a new flat-screen television, something my husband really wanted. At first, the splurge seemed overly indulgent to me; I didn't want to part with such a big chunk of money at once. After reviewing each of our spending patterns, we realized that my luxuries tend to be small, daily ones (such as those coffees and taxi rides). Similarly, I buy relatively inexpensive clothes on a somewhat regular basis. But Sujay doesn't spend much during the workday, and he rarely buys new clothes, preferring to make rare but larger purchases of pricier items, such as a new suit or shoes. So, we ended up deciding that spending so much on something he really wanted was fair, since it was balanced out by my more frequent, smaller purchases. Besides, I was getting a new television, too.

Q. Should I buy a hybrid car?

A. There are many reasons to purchase hybrid cars—they benefit the environment, save gas, and have even become a status symbol. But whether or not a hybrid will save you money depends on how much it costs, its fuel efficiency, the price of gas, and how often you drive. If you get in the car just once or twice a week, you might end up paying more for your hybrid than you save on gas.

To figure it out, try this simplified calculation: Subtract the price of a nonhybrid equivalent from the price of the hybrid you're considering. Set that number aside. Next, calculate how much you'll pay for gas with the nonhybrid by dividing the number of miles you drive each year by the car's EPA miles per gallon estimate. Then multiply that answer—the number of gallons you need each year—by the current price of gas. Do the same for the hybrid vehicle. Subtract those numbers from each other and you'll come up with your annual savings, which you should then multiply by the number of years you expect to keep the car to get your final answer. If it's greater than the price difference between the two cars, then go get your hybrid. (To make matters even more complex, some hybrids qualify for a tax credit, so that should enter your calculations as well.) Were you able to follow all that? If so, then congratulations are in order, because you're also a math genius.

When I asked Brent Kessel, a money manager in his early forties and author of *It's Not About the Money*, to keep a spending diary, it showed that he saved and spent money in a way that highlighted what he most valued. He considered installing a $499 Bluetooth phone system in his Audi, but he went with a $99 Motorola headset instead. He bought chairs at Macy's for $250 each instead of the $1,100 ones at Design Within Reach. But he doesn't deny himself everything—he installed a swimming pool in his backyard, because he had one when he was a kid. For him, having a pool is the "ultimate symbol of family fun," and seeing his kids and their friends play in it is well worth the price. His spending diary illuminated those priorities.

Personal finance expert and *You're So Money* author Farnoosh Torabi, thirty, applies a similar strategy: she developed guidelines for herself, such as eating one or two homemade meals each day to control costs. If she knows she's going out to dinner, she'll have breakfast at home. Her spending diary also shows a few splurges, including a $124 skirt and $80 shoes, but she continues to use them for television appearances related to her job.

The point of keeping a spending diary for a few days is not to stress over every $5 that leaves your wallet, but to make sure you're getting the most enjoyment out of each dollar spent. You might find that you worry too much about the $10 cab rides when the bigger waste is $100 dinners.

Budgeting is like cooking—as long as you approximate the amounts as well as you can, things will generally work out, and, once you establish some routines, then you don't even have to think about it anymore. My friend Annamarie, thirty-four, is the perfect example of this. She started waking up at 5:30 a.m. to make it to yoga class before her job as a government analyst begins. "It feels so great," she says. "Some mornings, I'm driving back home to get ready for work, and I just feel so happy." It costs $200 a month, and for Annamarie, it's worth it. "I don't feel pressure to 'have it all,' because I know I can't," she explains. She and her husband enjoy eating out, going on vacation, and owning nice furniture, so they do all those things, but they decided to delay buying their first home until they were expecting a baby in order to keep room for those other luxuries in their budget. Even as they were house hunting, they kept the budget for their mortgage low enough so they wouldn't have to give up those other pleasures. Because they both work hard in their jobs after years of having little money in graduate school, she thinks it's important for them to reward themselves. But that doesn't make her a squanderer. "When I decide to buy something, it's a pretty deliberate decision," she says. "But once I decide to buy it, I don't worry about it."

WINNING THE CONSUMER WARS

Retailers are willing to do almost anything, including deploying dubious tactics involving psychological trickery, to get us to spend money. To resist their charms, we need to understand their strategies.

Trick One: Luring us with a reward that's not as good as it sounds

I first suspected something strange was going on with credit card rewards when my friend Pegg whipped out her card one night to pay for dinner. "I almost have enough points to get an iPod," she explained.

It turns out that she isn't the only one who uses her credit card more than she otherwise would because of the rewards. Ran Kivetz, a Columbia University business professor, has found that people's motivation tends to increase as they get closer to goals, including those offered by credit card companies. He calls it "purchase acceleration."[4]

To test this theory, he looked at whether having a coffee reward card that gave people a free drink after ten purchases turned people into java junkies. (He conducted this study on the Columbia University campus, where coffee was clearly considered a valuable reward.) As participants got closer to receiving their free coffee, Kivetz found that the average length of time between their coffee purchases decreased. On average, people bought their ten coffees five days faster than they would have without the reward dangling in front of them.

That means that these so-called rewards could be inspiring us all to spend more than we would otherwise. And while buying a few extra cups of coffee won't break the bank, credit card rewards can be slightly more menacing. Since rewards cards come with higher interest rates than nonreward cards (on average, it's a difference of about two percentage points, or $200 a year on a $10,000 balance), then the 46 percent of consumers who don't pay off their balances each month are actually paying for the privilege of having the rewards cards.[5] Depending on the size of their balance, they might be paying more than they're getting in rewards. The only people who really get something for free are those who pay their balance in full each month. A handful of rewards cards, including certain airline-sponsored credit cards, also charge annual fees, which makes their rewards particularly costly, and usually not worth the price.

☑ Quick Tip: More Isn't Always Better

Think twice before buying in bulk. Research at Harvard Business School has found that paying a fee to shop at membership stores such as Sam's Club and Costco leads people to think they are saving money, even when they aren't. The researchers acknowledged that membership stores often sell bulk products at a discount; sometimes prices are as much as 10 percent below those at neighboring discount stores such as Walmart. But when they considered the membership fee, plus the fact that shoppers are likely to buy more than they otherwise would, they found that consumers ended up spending more money, not less. Plus, shoppers tended to end up with more lightbulbs or macaroni than they could ever possibly use.[6]

Trick Two: Putting us into a spending trance

Walk into a Sony Style store and you might catch a whiff of a sweetish scent with citrus bases and vanilla overtones. It's not from a teenage boy experimenting with aftershave. The company is trying to make its electronics less intimidating to women by puffing a slightly feminine smell at them, as well as to create a shopping environment so pleasurable that shoppers decide to linger for a few extra minutes (and perhaps walk out with a new laptop). The company's fragrance occasionally changes, depending on its marketing focus. For example, in the fall of 2009, Sony Style stores adopted a new bamboo scent to emphasize the company's green initiatives.

Research suggests that scents in retail environments work. A study by Washington State University's Eric Spangenberg found that certain smells—Rose Maroc in men's clothing stores and vanilla in women's—increased shopping time, the number of items purchased, and the amount spent. Music can have a similar effect, even if shoppers aren't aware of it.[7]

Retailers such as H&M and Zara use a related strategy. By frequently replacing the items in their store inventories with new choices, they have trained customers to buy clothes quickly, instead of waiting and thinking the decision over. (Shoppers worry that, if they delay their purchases, the items will no longer be for sale when they return.) Researchers at the University of Pennsylvania's Wharton School built a mathematical model suggesting that rapid turnover can boost profits by an average of 67 percent. One-day specials and midnight madness sales work the same way.[8]

Buying online is often a good idea. It's easier to compare prices at many stores at once, especially if you go to comparison websites such as pricegrabber.com. Even if you plan on making your purchase at a physical store, checking out your options ahead of time can save cash and prevent impulse buys. And if you do end up buying online, always look for discount codes first to avoid paying for shipping. Do a web search for the retailer's name combined with the term "coupon" or "free shipping," and chances are you'll find a discount code.

Trick Three: Leading us to believe that the posted price is the final price

As my husband and I were planning a romantic weekend away, I happened to be interviewing Linda Babcock, coauthor of *Ask for It: How Women Can Use the Power of Negotiation to Get What They Really Want.* (Despite the title, the advice applies to men as well.) Babcock told me that she had recently knocked 20 percent off of her total on a jewelry purchase simply by asking for a discount. As I did more research, I found that all kinds of retailers—Best Buy, Home Depot, department stores—were empowering their clerks to provide customers with discounts, but only when pressed. Shoppers simply had to start a conversation with a line such as "Is there any wiggle room with that price?" or "I saw that product on sale for less online; can you give me the same deal?" A few weeks later, at a farmers' market, I saved $30 when buying four Pashmina scarves just by asking the vendor, "Could I get a discount if I buy more than one?"

Ignore rebates, because if you are like the majority of purchasers, you will fail to send them in. In fact, research suggests that redemption rates generally fall below 50 percent, even for expensive items where the rebate would save the buyer $50 or more.[9] In a 2009 *Consumer Reports* survey, one in four people said that they never send in rebates, because the process involves too many steps, they lose their receipts, or they miss the deadline, or because of a variety of other reasons.[10] Not only do shoppers have to mail in the rebate form on time, but they also need to make note of when they expect to receive it and follow up with the company if it doesn't arrive. In addition, rebates often get "lost in the mail," partly because they arrive disguised as junk mail. So when shopping for products that come with rebates, assume you'll be paying the full price, unless you are extremely well organized.

The negotiating trend has become so prevalent that the advertising firm Cramer-Krasselt came up with a name for such pushy customers: neo-hagglers. The firm found that about half of consumers now try to negotiate prices on car repairs, appliances, and electronics, partly because the Internet makes it so easy to compare prices at different stores.

I tried my hand at this as I planned our weekend getaway to St. Michaels, Maryland, a quiet resort town on the Chesapeake Bay. When I looked up hotel prices online, the best I could find was $300 a night. I was looking to spend around $150, but I didn't want to compromise too much—I wanted a room with a view of the bay and a Jacuzzi. (It was just for one night, after all.) I called the spa resort that was my top choice and asked whether the hotel had any discounts available. The reservations agent put me on hold while she checked. When she came back, she asked if I had a particular room in mind, and I described my Jacuzzi-with-view desires. "We can give you that room for $160," she told me. I accepted. Two weeks later, we were soaking in the tub while gazing out at the bay.

Standing up to company errors requires tough negotiating skills. One year, I paid $1,100 in charges that were the result of company mistakes, including health insurance claim rejections and flex-spending denials. Companies regularly make mistakes on credit card statements, cell phone bills, and standard cash-register ring-ups. Bob Sullivan, author of *Gotcha Capitalism: How Hidden Fees Rip You Off Every Day—And What You Can Do About It*, found that complaining can pay off: complaints to credit card companies and airlines were successful at least 60 percent of the time.[11] Because correcting one mistake can take hours out of your workday, online complaints are often the best approach. Almost all companies now make it possible to either virtually chat with a sales rep or send an email, with many guaranteeing a response within forty-eight hours.

Taking control of everyday and special-occasion spending is what allows people like Kimberly Wilson and my friend Annamarie to spend money in a way that gets them toward their bigger goals, whether it's buying a cabin in West Virginia or maintaining a daily yoga practice. Sometimes, however, taking control also means focusing on the other end of the equation: how much money is coming in.

Exercises: Outsmarting Consumer Culture

1. Make a list of your big financial goals, along with an estimated timeline for achieving them. Keep the list handy and review it regularly.

2. Keep a spending diary for two weeks. Write down every single thing you spend money on, along with brief notes about why and how it made you feel. When the two weeks are over, review the list and see what surprises you.

3. Create a spending plan that maps out how much you want to put toward basic living costs (food, housing, and transportation), debt payments, savings, professional and household expenses, and entertainment.

Compare it to how much you are actually spending. Work on bringing the two lists into alignment.

4. Ask for a deal. Next time you're about to purchase something—from boutique clothing to a hotel room to jewelry—consider asking for a discount. You can start the conversation by asking, "Is there any wiggle room with that price?" or "I wanted to pay closer to X. Can you do that for me?"

5. Before buying anything over $100, research your options first. The more expensive it is, the more money you stand to save by researching. Comparison shopping starts with web searches. Look at review sites such as cnet.com and shopping blogs to see what others have said about the product you're considering buying. Then, browse sites like eBay, Amazon, pricegrabber.com, and overstock.com. You could find the same item for much less.

2

JOB JUGGLING

Even in the most prestigious and well-paying professions, job security has, for the most part, gone the way of fully funded pensions. That means we can't rely on receiving a steady paycheck every two weeks for thirty years the way many of our parents did. Instead, financial stability now comes from cultivating multiple sources of income through freelance work, starting up our own businesses, and investing in our primary careers by networking and honing our skills. We also can't forget about our chief source of income—our day jobs, whether they overlap with our longer-term career goals or not.

In this chapter, you'll learn how to do the following:

1. Cultivate a more secure income by diversifying your sources

2. Weigh the pros and cons of going into business for yourself

3. Decide if you're earning enough money (the answer is probably no)

MORE MONEY, FEWER PROBLEMS

"Hellooo, how are we doing today?" an energetic Chhayal Parikh asks the dozen mostly female participants who have come to her Body Pump class at the Fitness First gym in downtown Washington, DC. She turns up the throbbing music, adjusts her headset, and exhorts participants to keep a firm grip as they lift their weight bars to chest level. She's transformed from the professional videographer I know as my colleague at *US News & World Report* to a kinder, peppier version of *The Biggest Loser's* Jillian Michaels.

By teaching four to six classes a week on top of her full-time job as a videographer, Chhayal, who's in her early thirties, earns an additional $8,000 to $10,000 a year. When she was twenty, she decided to get certified as an instructor and today, even though she has a full-time professional job, she's glad she did. Earlier this year, when she got laid off and was briefly out of work, she immediately ramped up her teaching schedule to fill in some of that missing income. She also dreams of going into business for herself one day, perhaps by leading exercise classes for new moms. In the meantime, she's experimenting with other forms of income as well, such as making videos for nonprofits and trade associations and creating an iPhone application that will let people follow her workout routines on their own time.

At the moment, she's just trying to push her class to work harder. As the room grows sweatier and students start to grimace as they lift their weights, Chhayal calls out, "How low can you go? Come on! First set of singles, go!" Seeing her in her green and white tank top and with her curly hair held back with a black headband, you would never guess she's not a full-time aerobics instructor.

Brainstorm with your significant other, friends, and family members about what they could see you doing in five to ten years, other than your current work. It can help shake loose those latent thoughts that might be brewing in your own head.

Earning income through a variety of sources, a form of multi-streaming, serves as a self-protection device against an unpredictable labor market.[1] The average worker now holds ten different jobs between ages eighteen and thirty-six.[2] Some of those job changes are voluntary, but layoffs are also more common. And, age discrimination laws notwithstanding, many employers find ways to shed workers as they get older and become more expensive. Those who navigate their career paths most successfully often earn money outside their full-time jobs, which gives them a safety net as well as a longer-term plan for eventual self-employment.

"[Multistreaming] is more common now because the barriers are down. With the Web, you can make yourself look impressive to potential clients with samples and your bio," says Michelle Goodman, author of *My So-Called Freelance Life: How to Survive and Thrive as a Creative Professional for Hire.* Michelle, now forty-two, started earning income from multiple sources when she was twenty-four. She had been working as a book publicist in New York and, on a road trip to San Francisco, decided office life was too rigid for her. So she took on freelance writing while juggling personal-assistant and administrative work for self-employed people so she could still pay her bills. During her first year, she made $6,000 from her writing, but it soon grew into a healthy income.

If you're starting a business, you need a website. After noticing that many writers own domain names that are the same as their personal names as a way of promoting their work, I decided to try to do the same. I visited the domain name site godaddy.com and checked on the availability of kimberlypalmer.com. Unfortunately, GoDaddy told me that the site was taken, but it offered to place a back order on it for $18.99, which meant that I would have the chance to bid on it as soon as it became available. I signed up.

A few days before the domain name was scheduled to become available, I received an email from a stranger in Australia who claimed to own the site. He said he would sell it to me for $250. I ignored the email because (1) I suspected it might be a scam, and (2) I wasn't willing to pay $250. Around the same time, GoDaddy sent me an email to tell me that the site would be up for auction in a few days. Then, a few days later, I got another email from GoDaddy that said I'd been outbid for the site. (My $18.99 fee had included a $10 bid, and I hadn't bothered to raise that amount.)

I called GoDaddy to find out what had happened. Adam Dicker, vice president of the aftermarket for domain names, told me that the domain name had sold for $15—it turns out that kimberlypalmer.com was pretty cheap, especially for a name that hundreds of people worldwide must have. In retrospect, since I know how little it actually sold for, I wish I had bid more. My name is worth at least $25 to me. (Of course, it's possible that if I had raised my bid the other bidder would have raised his, and it would have sold for a lot more.) Instead, I purchased bykimberlypalmer.com, a name that seems suitable for a writer, for $10.

The lesson: Whether you're trying to buy the domain name for your business or personal brand (i.e., your name), decide how much you're willing to spend ahead of time, and place your bid just like you would when trying to purchase a mountain bike on eBay. That way you won't miss the opportunity to grab your domain name while it's cheap. If you don't get your top choice, consider alternatives, such as www.yourname.biz or www.yourprofession yourname.com.

When the economy started dipping in 2008 and 2009, Michelle was grateful for her diversified sources of funding. By then, her clients included ABC News, the *Seattle Times*, and book publishers. "With a full-time job, if you get laid off, that's the whole thing. But if I got laid off from one of mine, I would still have 60 or 50 percent of my income left," she says. Plus, during the workday, she gets to pad around her home office in her flip-flops while being trailed by her black Labrador, instead of donning a suit and high heels and commuting to the office.

Michelle recommends keeping a list of goals handy to help steer you toward the types of jobs you want. For example, if you want to start a freelance art photography business but are willing to earn extra money by taking on corporate clients, make sure the corporate clients don't take up all of your time. If you need to build a new website to help attract new customers, put that on your list of goals. And make sure you're getting paid what you're worth. Don't accept $30 an hour when the competitive rate is closer to $60. Since freelance clients aren't paying for health care or other benefits, the hourly rate should be higher than the one you might earn at a full-time job. Michelle says charging too little is a common rookie mistake.

In Gia Lipa's case, multistreaming success came through blogging—a much sought-after gig, but one that's usually harder than it sounds. Gia, forty-four, originally started the popular personal finance blog thedigeratilife.com to teach herself more about the Internet while she was working as a technical engineer in Silicon Valley. After doing some extensive networking with other bloggers, she started getting around 1,000 visits a day. She continued to grow her audience and now earns around $10,000 a month through ads, links, and blog-related consulting, and she's since quit her day job to keep up. Jim Wang, thirty, has a similar story: He started bargaineering.com, where he writes about how to live more frugally—a topic that garnered a lot of interest during the recent recession. He earns about the same amount as Gia, which has allowed him to leave his software developing job to work full-time on his blog out of his home in Columbia, Maryland.

But blogging success doesn't happen easily, or quickly. Most blogs have fewer loyal fans than family Christmas letters and earn pennies per month, if anything. An online survey by Problogger found that the majority of bloggers earn less than $100 a month, and three in ten earn under $10 a month. Just 17 percent of respondents said they made enough to live on, or over $2,500 a month.[3] The ones who end up earning a living through their blogs typically network intensely in order to build up traffic, and they also figure out how to get their blogs to generate money beyond the usual Internet advertisements. By selling her blogging services and expertise to outside sites and companies, Gia generates about a third of her overall income. Another successful website owner, Kimberly Seals-Allers, founder of mochamanual.com, a site for moms of color, also sells related books, clothes, and consulting services. In addition, she licenses the Mocha Manual name for use in an instructional DVD that's sold at Walmart and supermarkets.

☑ Quick Tip: Earning Extra on the Side

Here are more ways to earn money outside your regular paycheck:
- **Offer your services on craigslist.org.** Whether your skills lie in editing, woodworking, web design, or juggling, people in your local area will likely pay for them. Post an ad and see who bites.
- **Start a small business.** People are willing to pay for dog-walking, house-cleaning, cooking, and even closet organization services. If you have an idea for a product that you think will sell—perhaps the next "Slanket" concept is brewing in your head—then make it, set up a website, and start marketing. You can start by performing a few services or giving away a few products to help spread the word and get endorsements, which you can then post on your website or blog. Next, consider advertising in the local paper or through local web forums.

- **Sell your wit.** Cafepress.com is one of the growing number of websites that allow users to design T-shirts and then sell them for a profit. The most successful designers tend to be the ones that quickly take advantage of trends with clever slogans. For example, after Tom Cruise jumped on Oprah's coach, "Free Katie" shirts became top sellers. After Vice President Joe Biden made an enthusiastic verbal gaffe after the passage of health care reform, shirts emblazoned with "Health insurance reform is a big #@%*! deal" immediately popped up on the site.
- **Get paid to talk.** Colleges and organizations like to hire people recognized as experts. To build up your portfolio, offer to speak for free as much as possible and get in the public eye by penning an op-ed or two. Once you have developed your resume, a speakers' association can help you find gigs and negotiate your rate. (Visit the National Speakers Association at nsaspeaker.org for more information.)
- **Teach.** If you're a writer, for example, look into teaching a workshop through a local writers' center or at a local community college. If you practice yoga, consider getting your teaching certification.
- **Make jewelry, stationery, soap, or other crafty items and sell them online.** Websites like etsy.com make it easy to set up shop.
- **Become a consultant.** If you're employed as an economist or in another profession with specialized skills, consider offering them up to companies on a contractual basis.

FLYING SOLO

When Tim Bradley, twenty-nine, and his wife, Anne Morrison Bradley, twenty-seven, started brainstorming about the kind of business they could start, they thought about what they love. They settled on two things: their dogs and design. While checking out the current offerings in the world of pet decor, they discovered that, for the most part, existing stores catered to what Anne and Tim call a "Paris Hilton aesthetic"—not a style they'd ever apply to their own home. They guessed that other shoppers, especially men, probably felt the same way. "If you took pride in your room, [the products sold by most stores] wouldn't fit," says Anne. The couple decided that there was a need for upscale, modern design products for people with pets that they could fill.

While Tim was finishing law school and Anne was working in corporate development in Ferndale, Michigan, they hired a graphic designer, formed a company, and built their website (thepremiumpet.com), for a total start-up cost of around $5,000. Anne thought of the slogan "Best friends deserve great design" to go with the business name, The Premium Pet. By using their tax refund money, they avoided debt, which helped Anne get past her fear of taking such a big risk.

☑ Quick Tip: Tax Time

If you start to spend money on business-related start-up costs, such as books, a new computer, or dog crates, then you can usually deduct those costs on your tax return. Be sure to keep track of what you spend and store receipts in a file that will be easy to find when you do your taxes.

Within a few months, Anne and Tim started contacting vendors who might be interested in working with them. They planned to buy the vendors' products at wholesale prices and then sell them to customers for a profit. Since they work out of a spare bedroom in their house, with files, two dogs, and computers spread around the room, they don't have much storage space. So, by setting up a system for "drop shipping," where Anne and Tim transfer the customer's order information to the vendor, who would then ship the products directly to the customer, they anticipated minimizing their overhead costs and storage requirements.

They found plenty of vendors who were interested in working with them, since Anne and Tim were taking care of the advertising and getting the products in front of potential customers. While holding on to their full-time day jobs (Tim had since graduated and begun working as a patent attorney), they spent an extra ten to twenty hours a week, usually during lunch hours and in the evenings, recruiting vendors and getting the rest of the company ready for launch.

Q. I get paid part of my salary in cash. Do I have to pay taxes on that amount?
A. Yes. While it might be tempting to pocket the cash you receive as part of your new business, you must pay taxes on that income. Not only is it wrong not to pay taxes but you also have a decent chance of getting caught. The IRS audits taxpayers both randomly and in a targeted way, in an effort to track down the roughly $300 billion in taxes that are not paid each year. For some cash-intensive jobs, such as waiting tables, the IRS uses statistics to estimate expected income, and any difference between that and the actual amount reported could trigger an audit.

Anne and Tim launched the company in 2009 and plan to wait several years before paying themselves, choosing instead to reinvest the money into advertising and other improvements. Their goal is to earn enough to give them more flexibility in their careers. Although Tim doesn't plan on quitting his legal job anytime soon, Anne would like to leave her position when they have kids, so she can grow the business from home. Eventually, they would like to move to North Carolina to be near Tim's sister, who launched the now multimillion-dollar children's decor company Rosenberry Rooms, which serves as a model for Tim and Anne's business. In ten years, Tim says, "We would love to just be able to work for ourselves."

They're not the only ones. Chelsea Rippey, a Utah-based mother and home decorator in her early thirties, decided to start her own business in October 2004 after feeling frustrated with the clothing options available to her and other Mormons. "I found it really difficult to find styles that would work with my modesty standards. . . . It was hard to find anything that allowed me to be both comfortable and fashionable," she says. She started by designing an undershirt that could be worn beneath other clothes to cover up key body parts. She didn't start out with a fashion background, but she taught herself how to design and select fabrics. She's since hired specialists to help her, and her company, Shade Clothing, now sells dresses, maternity clothes, and bathing suits alongside tops and bottoms.

Chelsea had tapped into a growing trend that extended well beyond the Mormon market. Soon, Macy's was interested in her designs, and she also had more competition from start-ups like her own. Within two years, the company was selling almost nine million dollars' worth of clothes a year and employing over one hundred people.

Tim, Anne, and Chelsea are among the increasing number of young entrepreneurs who are often motivated by a desire to have more control over their lives. But, even though the number is growing, young people still tend to be underrepresented among small-business owners. The self-employment rate for all ages hovers around 11 percent, but it's just 5.6 percent for people in their late twenties and climbs to around 8 percent for those in their early thirties.[4]

☑ Quick Tip: Scheduling Creativity

Getting creative can help reinvigorate a job that has become stale. Todd Henry, founder of the Accidental Creative, an online forum and podcast, says exposing your mind to new types of experiences can help it to think outside the box. He suggests reading a magazine you would never normally look at—a software engineer might want to pick up a copy of Vogue, for example. "You need to be intentional about experiencing new things in your life," he says. He also recommends managing your energy. If you find meetings to be draining, then take time out in between them, or try to schedule fewer of them. Make sure you block out time that's just for you, and defend it if necessary. If you're most creative from 8 a.m. to 10 a.m., then tell people you are unavailable during that time. Because you are—you're busy thinking.

The Bureau of Labor Statistics points out that younger people may lack the funds and skills to start up a business. But having less to lose also coincides with a higher tolerance for risk, and there are usually ways to find funding for the new venture. Tim Ferriss, author of *The 4-Hour Workweek* and entrepreneur himself, dismisses the lack of capital and experience as "excuses," whether they're used at age twenty or sixty. "I don't think those are insurmountable obstacles at all. If you look at Steve Wozniak, Steve Jobs, Michael Dell, Bill Gates—any number of hundreds of companies that are household names were all started by people with no capital and no experience. Having little capital and little experience can be very helpful because, one, you don't know what's impossible, and, two, you make deliberate, smart decisions rather than misspending money."

Pamela Skillings, career coach and author of *Escape from Corporate America*, agrees. "It can be really useful to work for somebody else for a couple years, but I don't think you need to wait until you're wealthy. . . . When you're younger, you have the energy and passion and that means so much when you're starting a business, even more so than having the capital," she says. Skillings started her own career-coaching business when she was in her early thirties, while still working in her corporate marketing job.

If you need another reason, consider this: on average, salaried workers who don't work for the government or in agriculture earn $39,635. Compare that to the nonagricultural self-employed average salary of $53,939.[5] (Of course, when you calculate your projected earnings, you'll want to take into account additional expenses—or savings—that come from working for yourself, such as paying for your own health insurance.) Even if you still hang on to your day job, like Tim Bradley, having an additional source of income gives you greater financial security, and an automatic backup plan just in case that primary job suddenly disappears.

Career coach Pamela Skillings calls the delicate balance of working a full-time job while pursuing another interest on the side "ethical moonlighting." Basically, you need to follow the necessary rules so you don't end up getting fired from your day job while exploring other options. Skillings says that the key is to continue excelling during the day. That means avoiding the temptation to spend your mornings writing up your own business plan while you're being paid to advance your team project. (She points out that companies often monitor employee emails and phone calls.) She also recommends keeping quiet about your outside work—there's no reason to draw attention to the fact that your true passions are focused elsewhere. Reviewing company policies on outside work can also be useful; some firms prohibit blogging or other public activities. Lastly, Skillings recommends steering clear of conflicts of interest by making sure you're not stealing clients or working for a competitor.

THE MAIN GIG

When I was starting out in journalism, I was pretty much convinced that money didn't matter to me at all. I just wanted to be happy, and writing made me happy. Of course, I quickly realized how wrong I was. I wanted to go on vacations, buy dresses from Anthropologie, and pay rent each month without worrying that I was close to emptying out my checking account. So before going in for a final interview for one of my first jobs, I practiced asking for more money with my dad.

During our practice sessions, my dad played the role of my future boss.

"So, Kimberly, we would like to offer you $34,000," he said.

"Um, would $40,000 work?" I said feebly.

My dad interrupted. "You have nothing to be ashamed of. Just ask for more, in a clear voice. Try, 'I am really eager to work here, but I was hoping to earn $40,000,'" he suggested.

I tried it his way. I felt awkward. I dreaded the actual encounter when I'd be talking to my future boss instead of my dad. I was sure he wouldn't be as friendly (or as helpful).

During the actual interview, that future boss appeared to feel as awkward as I did over the negotiations, which apparently worked in my favor, because he ended up offering me close to what I asked for. And, since all my future raises were based on that initial conversation, I think I've already netted at least $25,000 from those practice sessions with my dad. Asking for more money early in one's career can mean the difference of half a million dollars over the course of one's lifetime, according to Linda Babcock and Sara Laschever, authors of *Ask for It.* (They also report that men are four times more likely than women to negotiate their first salary, which contributes to the gender income gap.[6])

Q. My friends all make more money than I do. How do I not resent them?

A. Go ahead, resent them a little. It can help you figure out just what it is you're lusting after. Is it their financial security? Their job? The fact that their kitchen looks like a Williams Sonoma ad? Envy can actually be a useful tool for figuring out what choices you should be making.

But don't get too worked up, because chances are, they're not doing as well as they seem to be. Shira Boss, author of *Green with Envy*, says that people often don't realize the amount of debt that goes into supporting people's lifestyles, although she adds that the mortgage crisis helped shed some light on that. "Because most people don't talk openly about money issues, especially money stress, we're fooled into thinking it must just be we who are struggling, when in fact it's most people," she says. Shira also recommends shifting your perspective: instead of comparing yourself to those who appear to have more, consider those who have less, and be grateful.

When negotiating your salary, don't forget to consider benefits. Health insurance coverage can be worth thousands of dollars a year, and so can maternity and paternity benefits. Pensions and matching programs for 401(k)s also automatically increase the value of your salary package. A survey by the Transamerica Center for Retirement Studies found that people tend to make the mistake of prioritizing a larger salary over better benefits, and this choice can cost them in the long run.[7]

There is a good chance that you could be earning more money than you are right now, especially if you didn't negotiate at the start of your employment or if you've been less than aggressive in asking for pay raises. Even if you chose your career more for its psychic income than the paycheck, you still deserve to be paid for your hard work. Even though we increasingly rely on earning income from multiple sources, the bulk of our salaries will likely come from a single source for a significant period of time. Maximizing it is one of the single most important steps we can take toward improving our financial situation. Another important step is to keep that main salary. Side jobs provide a safety net, but that day job is the tightrope, and it gives you the time and resources to be able to explore other, perhaps more interesting, opportunities.

Getting Ahead

Sometimes, knowing how to excel isn't that easy. When career expert Alexandra Levit started out in the corporate world after college, she made the mistake of thinking that if she worked really hard she would get promoted. "But the business world is not that simple. It's more based on relationships with people and the visibility that you generate for yourself and what people think about what you're doing. What people think of you is much more important than the work product or the amount you're churning out. As a result, I had several setbacks where I would watch people with half my work product get promoted because people knew who they were. They were out there, networking," she says.

To rectify that situation, she took a Dale Carnegie course in personal development. It taught her cooperation, diplomacy, how to be more assertive, and how to relate to people. "I came into my own," says Alexandra, who wrote a book, *They Don't Teach Corporate in College*, about her experience. "I finally started getting promoted."

Sometimes, a career coach or development course can help you get "unstuck." Talk about your goals for the session ahead of time to make sure you get what you want out of it. (The price of one-on-one coaching typically starts at around $200 an hour.[8] Occasionally, companies foot the bill, and some coaches offer more leeway on their pricing for clients who are paying their own way.) Less formal advice can come from meeting with more experienced colleagues and mentors over lunch or coffee; they will often be happy to talk with you.

Going out to lunch with a colleague or client can come with dozens of potential pitfalls, including what to wear, how to greet the person, and how to handle the check. Judith Bowman, protocol consultant and author of *Don't Take the Last Donut: New Rules of Business Etiquette*, says the key to making a lunch go smoothly is to remember that you're there to get to know each other outside of an office environment, and not to eat. For that reason, she suggests delaying any discussion of business until dessert or coffee, unless the other person brings it up sooner. "Get to know them, build trust, and grow the relationship," she says. To avoid the awkward jostling over who pays, she recommends giving your credit card to the restaurant ahead of time so the check is never seen. (And, by the way, if you did the asking, then you should be the one paying.) She also suggests ordering food that is similar to what your companion orders, so he's not watching you chow down on salad while he waits for his main course. Here are some of her other suggestions:

- If you arrive first, wait to be seated until your lunch date arrives.
- Ignore traditional gender roles: women shouldn't hesitate to open doors, walk to the table behind their guest, and get the check.
- Order before getting deeply embroiled in conversation, in order to avoid an overly long lunch.
- Don't order the most expensive or least expensive item on the menu.
- Pay attention to your manners; they make an impression.
- Avoid ordering pizza, ribs, and other messy dishes.

As you climb the ladder at your main job, it can get harder to set time aside for your small business idea or blog. But carving out a few hours a week, or ten minutes a day, can keep you sane, in addition to setting the groundwork for a career shift later.

Exercises: Are You Making Enough Money?

1. Make a list of all of the ways that you could earn money outside of your current job. What talents do you have that you'd like to sell? Do you daydream about organizing desks or designing T-shirts? Keep that list nearby so that if you want to act on it—or if you need to in the event of a job loss—you're ready. Brainstorm with a friend or family member for more ideas.

2. Take small steps toward multistreaming your income. Pick an item on your list and get started, perhaps with a small step such as purchasing a domain name. Maybe you'll make just $500 this year, or maybe it will just be an investment year and you'll make nothing. Either way, being able to earn money from sources other than your main job will give you more freedom, as well as peace of mind.

3. Do you know how your salary compares to that of your peers? Do some research on salary comparison websites, such as salary.com or payscale.com. If the estimates seem way off base—which they can, especially if you have an unusual job or one with a difficult-to-understand title—then dig deeper. If you're close to a coworker, then ask that person what he or she thinks the pay range should be for a variety of jobs at your workplace to get a sense of how you stack up. If you both feel comfortable, feel free to share your salaries, but be prepared for the inevitable gnawing feeling in your stomach if you come up short—and be ready to act on it. It can be equally awkward if it turns out you earn more.

4. Practice talking about money. Part of the reason people hesitate to ask for raises is that they feel uncomfortable talking about finances. To get in the habit, ask friends about how they negotiated their salaries or how often they have asked for raises. There's no need to talk hard numbers or put anyone on the spot. Just explain that you're looking to learn how to broach the subject at work.

5. Consider asking for a raise. If more than a year has passed since your last pay increase—or if you discover that you are underpaid compared to your peers—then it's time to make your case. Write a memo that outlines why you deserve a raise, including the contributions you've made over the last year, and ask for a specific dollar amount. If your research

suggests that it's warranted, don't hesitate to ask for a 10 to 20 percent increase. Run the request and your reasons by a trusted friend or family member and rehearse how you plan to bring it up. Then, forward the memo to your boss and ask for a meeting to discuss it. Once you get in there, briefly summarize your points, make your request, and be prepared to discuss your boss's concerns. (Keep in mind that there are a few situations in which asking for a raise might not be appropriate: if your workplace has been laying people off or has recently lost a big source of income, or if your industry is going through a downturn that makes you grateful to have any job, then postpone the monetary requests until the storm passes.)

6. When you switch jobs, you have the most power to negotiate. You may not get another one for a while, so don't miss the opportunity to make the request before accepting the position. After receiving the job offer, express your enthusiasm and gratitude. Then, politely say that the amount was a bit less than you had expected and if they could consider raising the offer by X amount, you would appreciate it. (Even if the salary range was clearly stated in the job posting, there is often still room for negotiation.) Then stop talking. Silence helps encourage them to change their offer. Even if you have received an offer that exceeds your expectations, you may still want to consider asking for an additional 5 to 10 percent. It could be your last chance for years.

3

THE UPSIDE OF DEBT

Ever since subprime mortgages were blamed for causing the largest economic slowdown since the Great Depression, debt's reputation has slid downhill. But, in certain situations, debt can be very healthy. Student loans and, in some cases, using credit cards, can catapult a person into the next stage of her career. Professional clothing, night classes, the services of a career consultant—these can all be paid for through loans. Meanwhile, exposure to the dark side of debt, including fees and interest payments, can be limited through careful management. Making debt work for you instead of against you just requires some advance planning and a little research.

In this chapter, you'll learn how to do the following:

1. Evaluate debt opportunities and calculate their true cost, financial and otherwise

2. Decide whether to pay off a student loan or invest the money instead

3. Beat financial institutions at their own game by learning how to use the system to your advantage

SMOOTH TALKER

On one of our early dates in a smoky student bar on the University of Chicago's campus, Sujay, my future husband, explained the theory of income smoothing to me. (For two graduate students, this counted as flirting.) Basically, he said, living well off of loans while in school or otherwise underemployed makes sense, because you'll soon be earning money again, when you can pay back what you borrowed and never feel like you sacrificed too much of the good life. At the time, our definition of living well didn't mean much more than avoiding ramen noodles and seeing the occasional movie, but his theory did enable us to have some fancy first dates at sushi bars and Turkish restaurants. (For us, though, it seems to have worked in reverse because, after getting married and getting jobs, we eat at decidedly less upscale places than we did on those first dates.)

The income smoothing theory requires some level of comfort with debt, a financial tool that has become unpopular over the last several years as credit card users have been increasingly portrayed as less responsible than the stars of MTV's reality shows. But in many ways, debt's name has been unfairly maligned. The ability to borrow money can give us power—the power to get an education, live in a house, pay for groceries when we're temporarily unemployed, and an infinite number of other possibilities. Even Carmen Wong Ulrich, author of *Generation Debt*, acknowledges that debt can be a wonderful thing. In fact, it's what enabled her to support herself after she graduated from college. "Money for the futon had to come from somewhere. . . . I had to start my career and I couldn't live at home, so I needed a place to sleep, and a couple good outfits to go on job interviews," she says. As the daughter of immigrants, Carmen says she knows what it's like to start from nothing. "I really appreciate that debt has gotten me to where I am today, and I had access to borrow funds. As much as I write about debt, I don't think it's a monstrosity.

It can be a tool," she says. (After finding work, she paid off her credit card debt quickly, by focusing on the highest-interest cards first.)

Not all debt is equal, of course, and whether taking it on is a good or bad idea depends on the kind, how expensive it is, and how it fits in with the rest of your financial life. The answers to those questions are often masked by myths that have been ingrained in us: that all student loan debt is "good debt;" that all credit card debt is bad; and that we shouldn't take on debt for anything that doesn't provide a return, like a home.

Student loans tend to be the cheapest form of debt, partly because they are often subsidized by the federal government. But the growth of the private loan industry in recent years means that many students graduate with some of their loans locked into interest rates that are over 10 percent, which can make them as toxic as credit card debt. Auto loans also tend to be relatively cheap, partly because they are sometimes subsidized by dealerships and manufacturers. Credit card debt is usually the most expensive, although it varies widely; those who know how to cleverly navigate the world of plastic may be able to pay close to nothing for the money they are borrowing.

In general, debt levels go up with education levels, which means that young professionals carry much larger debt burdens than those in other groups do. (Of course, we are also more likely to have the income to be able to manage our debt.) The average adult with a college degree has almost $10,000 in credit card debt, while high school graduates carry around $6,000. Type of career also has an influence: households headed by someone in a managerial or professional position carry an average of $9,948 in credit card debt compared to $5,827 for those with heads of households in technical, sales, or service-related fields, according to a Demos analysis of the latest Survey of Consumer Finances.[1]

Your credit score determines how much you will pay for a mortgage, car loan, or any other type of loan. Lenders interpret your score as a measure of how risky it is to lend money to you. So you want to make sure it's as high as possible. (Anything above a 720 is typically considered excellent.) Here's how:

- **Get your free credit report** at annualcreditreport.com, the central website run by all three credit bureaus, Experian, TransUnion, and Equifax, once a year. Don't be fooled by other sites, such as freecreditreport.com, which automatically enrolls you in a costly credit monitoring program. (Credit scores, different from credit reports, cost around $15 to obtain from the credit bureaus, but there's usually no need to get your actual score as long as you get your free credit report.)

- **Fix any mistakes that you see.** If you see an address on your report that's not yours, or anything else that looks unfamiliar, contact the credit bureaus to let them know what's wrong. They are required by law to correct errors. Keep a record of your interactions in case you need to follow up.

- **Defend your identity.** Seeing a charge on a credit statement or getting a bill in the mail that's not yours is often the first sign that your identity has been stolen. If anything is amiss, contact your card company and the credit bureaus right away.

- **Don't pay anyone to improve your credit score.** Dozens of companies advertise on the radio and in newspapers that they can help you improve your score. Not only are they expensive, but some of their techniques border on fraudulent.

- **Don't cancel cards.** Although it's counterintuitive, canceling a credit card actually temporarily decreases your credit score, so if you're close to taking out a new loan, keep all your cards in play. You don't need to put charges on them, but keep the accounts open.

- **Stick with the basics.** By paying your bills on time, staying well under your credit limits, and keeping accounts in good standing over many years, you will steadily improve your score.

Let's return for a moment to our average young professional, Kenneth, whom we met in chapter 1. He still has some residual credit card debt from his college years, as well as $30,000 in student loans and a $10,000 car loan, so his interest payments add up to about $2,250 a year—and that's just the interest. This number doesn't even include the payments that go toward the principal. The breakdown looks like this:[2]

Cost of student loans ($30,000 with a 3 percent interest rate): $900
Cost of car loan ($10,000 with a 6 percent interest rate): $600
Cost of credit card loans ($5,000 with a 15 percent interest rate): $750

Kenneth often wonders whether he should use some of his savings to pay off chunks of his debt. The answer depends on how much his savings are earning in interest compared to his loan interest rates and whether he wants to keep the cash available for other reasons. In general, he'll be better off paying down the loans that are costing him more than he is earning on his savings. For example, if he paid off his credit card loan, it would give him an automatic 15 percent return compared to letting that money sit in a non-interest-bearing checking account. Since most of his savings are in a money market fund earning around 4 percent in interest a year, he should pay off his car loan and credit card debt if he has the extra cash.

The decision is also influenced by what he wants to do with his money over the next five to ten years. If he plans to make a major career change or take time out of the workforce, he might opt to make minimum payments on his debt so he can hold on to his savings. Kenneth doesn't plan on leaving his job, but he does want to buy a home, so he's keeping as much cash on hand as possible for that down payment. But he also wants to unload expensive debt, since those monthly payments will limit the size of the mortgage he can take on. So Kenneth is paying off his expensive credit card debt as quickly as possible and aims to pay off his car loan over the next two years, so it will be gone by the time he and his wife, Danielle, are ready to buy their condo. He'll let his student loan, on the other hand, stick around, since he's earning more in interest than the loan is costing him.

NOTHING COMES BETWEEN ME AND MY STUDENT LOANS

If you're a young professional, chances are you're carrying student loan debt. The latest numbers from the College Board show that 60 percent of students who graduate with bachelor's degrees carry loan debt, which ranges from an average of $18,800 for public university graduates to $23,800 for private school graduates.[3] (Those averages exclude those who graduate debt free.) That's a lot of money for someone who has yet to start his career. Debt loads for those finishing up law school, med school, and other graduate programs are even heftier.

So when should you pay it off? Does it make sense to continue living like a poor student for a few years while you funnel all extra money toward the financial institutions you're beholden to, or should you celebrate your newfound employment with a decent apartment and social life while making just the minimum payments? Mitch Wrosch, a twenty-nine-year-old attorney in Los Angeles, found himself facing that question after graduating from Wayne State University Law School in Michigan. He currently puts about $1,300 a month toward his student loan debt of roughly $130,000. (That amount also includes about $20,000 from his undergrad days and $13,000 for his living expenses while he studied for the bar.) His interest rates range from 3.8 percent to 7.9 percent, which makes them relatively inexpensive, but probably worth paying off since it's unlikely he could reliably earn as high a rate from a savings account to offset those interest payments.

In the short term, Mitch plans to continue making his monthly payments without paying off any big chunks at once. He took graduate school courses in Israel before settling into his law career and doesn't expect to have extra cash available to him anytime soon. But if and when he does, say in ten years, then he plans to pay off his student loans before putting the money toward other investments. "Living with a crushing amount of debt is not enjoyable. The peace of mind I would have from living debt free is more valuable to me than trying to maximize my investments," he says.

Q. My parents always say my student loan debt is good debt, so I don't need to worry about paying it off. Is that really true?

A. Parents enjoy calling it "good" debt because they are happy that it is helping you to advance your career. So in that sense, it's "good." And loans that are subsidized by the federal government and locked in at very low interest rates are also good. But some private student loans are as expensive as credit card debt. So make sure you know what your interest rates are, and pay off the higher-interest-rate debt as quickly as possible. Even subsidized federal loans can leave you paying hundreds of dollars a month or more once you graduate, and thinking of it as "good" debt won't be much consolation when it prevents you from buying a house or car. Debt that pays for a law degree that you don't really want isn't "good debt" either, so make sure you're studying something that you'll enjoy applying in the real world for the next thirty-plus years.

There are other ways of lessening the burden. You can be excused from your federal loans, at least for a period, if your monthly payments are greater than 20 percent of your gross income, you're completing an internship, or you're suffering from some kind of debilitating personal problem. Returning to school can also qualify you for deferment.[4] (However, in most cases, the interest continues to build on the loans, so delaying repayment should only be used as a last resort.)

The Debt-Free Life

Gregory Go, the thirty-three-year-old cofounder of the personal finance site wisebread.com, started living debt free after paying off the $10,000 of credit card debt he had built up during college. It took him three years of making small payments while working a $10-an-hour help-desk technician job, but it felt so good that he's avoided taking on any new debt since. He makes do with a fifteen-year-old Honda Civic and lives with a roommate—but he says he doesn't feel like he's sacrificing. When he compares his situation to that of friends with new cars and homes, he says, "I look at them and I don't want to be in their shoes. Some friends bought homes at their peak, and now are regretting it." He adds that he's had inklings of jealousy in the past, but he'd still rather live debt free than be in their situation. As for his social life, it hasn't suffered. He hosts potlucks and game nights, which means he gets to spend time with friends for a fraction of the cost of a night out. As an added bonus, he tends to clean out his friends' wallets in poker games.

When it comes to loan forgiveness, the Holy Grail for student borrowers, the rules are changing. Under the federal program created by the 2007 College Cost Reduction and Access Act, borrowers can sign up to pay only a certain percentage of their monthly discretionary income—no more than 15 percent—toward their loans. If the loans still haven't been paid off after 25 years, the remainder is forgiven. Certain professions, such as law enforcement, social work, and teaching, come with the added benefit of loan forgiveness after ten years. (This program only applies to federal loans, not private ones.)

Even filing for bankruptcy doesn't discharge your student loans. That's a good reason to compare average starting salaries of graduates in the field before returning to school. As the recession took hold in 2008 and 2009, many recent grads were wishing they weren't looking for work while carrying around $200,000 of debt from getting advanced degrees, even allegedly lucrative ones, such as MBAs.

☑ **Quick Tip: Student Loan Scrutiny**

If you're considering going back to school, take this advice from New York's attorney general Andrew Cuomo, who exposed the shady deals that universities were making with lenders in 2007: "Caveat emptor. Let the buyer beware. When you sign these loan documents, you are signing what is the equivalent of an education mortgage. It can be in excess of $100,000. You're paying for it for years and years. It will affect your credit rating. It's one of the most important financial decisions a young person is going to make. Inform yourself. Do not rely solely on the recommendations of the college."[5]

OUTSMARTING THE CREDIT CARD COMPANY

Credit card companies have become the bogeyman of debt. They have a reputation for being unfair, changing rules frequently to exact maximum suffering, and, ultimately, being evil. But that's not completely fair. Carmen Wong Ulrich isn't the only one who credits plastic with improving her lifestyle. Curtis Arnold, founder of the credit card information site cardratings.com and father of six, financed his family's minivan purchase at no cost by charging it to a card that offered a zero percent introductory rate for one year. While most card companies count on some portion of consumers to either make late payments or carry debt past the introductory period in order to turn a profit, Curtis was careful to transfer the $13,000 balance to a credit card that offered another teaser rate within the twelve months. (He also initially charged the purchase to his Discover card, which gave him about 1 percent cash back, or $130. Then, he transferred the balance to the card with the zero percent rate. So he got free financing and an extra discount.) Without his credit card, Curtis would have been at the mercy of the dealership's financing terms, which would have cost him about 6 percent in annual interest. He used a similar technique to pay for his wedding. "I believe any time credit card companies throw out these carrots, in the form of a zero percent rate for twelve months or six months, you can learn how to use these offers in a savvy manner," says Curtis. (He adds that, after the worldwide financial crisis, it's more difficult to make credit card transfers to cards with teaser rates without incurring fees, so consumers should be sure to do their research ahead of time.)

Credit cards come with other advantages, too. They offer free protection from identity theft and retailers who mistakenly double-charge you. They can give you rewards, in the form of airline miles, cash back, or other gifts. And they let you track your monthly spending far more easily than you could with cash. As long as you're among the 54 percent of people who pay off their balances each month, review your statement each time it arrives, and complain within sixty days of seeing an error, it's hard to see credit cards as anything other than useful.[6] Some of these benefits, such as the ability to track your spending, also come with debit cards, which subtract money directly out of your checking account. But debit cards generally don't offer rewards or as much fraud protection, and they don't help you build your credit score. That's why consumers who have their debt under control usually benefit from using credit cards.

The landmark credit card legislation of 2009, most of which went into effect in early 2010, makes it even easier for consumers to use credit cards to their advantage. Companies now have to give customers more warning if they raise fees, which they can only do if customers are late in paying their bills and in a handful of other circumstances. They also have to make it easier for them to pay off their higher-interest debt first, and they must word their policies using clearer language.

If you carry any debt at all, then there's only one factor you need to consider: the interest rate. Because cards with rewards are typically about two percentage points higher than those without rewards, you want to minimize interest payments by selecting the cheapest card.[7] (Interest rates don't matter if you pay off your balance each month, since you're not paying any interest.) You can use websites such as cardratings.com, creditcards.com, or indexcreditcards.com for quick comparisons.

The next factor to consider is the annual fee, which you want to avoid. Most credit cards don't have them, so there's no need to pay one. The one exception is if you have your eye on an exclusive rewards-heavy card, such as the platinum, gold, or green American Express cards. The rewards that come with those cards are impressive, including private meet-and-greets with celebrities and luxury hotel stays. And if you're spending tens of thousands of dollars a year on your credit card, then a few hundred dollars of annual fees probably mean about as much to you as a small coffee does to most people.

Many cards come with more routine rewards, ranging from spa certificates to jewelry. There's nothing wrong with benefiting from them, as long as you're not paying any interest or annual fees on the card—in that case, the cost would likely cancel out the value of any free gift. If you are paying interest, then you might be tempted to sign up for one of these cards, reap some quick rewards, and then cancel the card before the interest builds up, but canceling cards brings its own punishment, in the form of a temporarily diminished credit score. It doesn't make intuitive sense that canceling a card would ding your credit, but it does. That means a canceled credit card could make it more expensive for you to take out a car loan or a home mortgage. In general, the cost of a higher interest rate on those types of major loans far outweighs any potential credit card rewards.

Other benefits, such as warranties and travel insurance, vary by card, as do fees charged on international transactions, which will add up for frequent travelers. You also want to look into how easy it is to make payments online. Many people like to use a credit card issued by the same bank where they have their other accounts for easy transfers.

NOT EVERYONE'S A DEBT-AVOIDING ROCK STAR

Sometimes, life events conspire against you and you find yourself wondering if you'll ever get back on track. One thirty-something reader of my blog wrote to me after she had lost her job, been in an accident requiring $40,000 of surgery, and started a business that went on to fail. "I went from a 700 credit score and money to spare to having $100,000 debt, little to no income, and Chapter 7 bankruptcy," she said. She had to move back home with her parents as she picked up the pieces. "I feel like I threw my life away," she wrote.

Recovering from debt overload is always a struggle, but one that usually has an end in sight. The first step is to see if there's any way to pay off all of the accumulated debt. With credit cards, starting with the ones that are close to surpassing (or have surpassed) their credit limits will eliminate further monthly fees building up and increased interest payments. The next priority is paying off the highest-interest cards first, since they're costing the most. You might also want to consider transferring the debt to the lowest-interest-rate card, but first make sure the transfer fee doesn't exceed the amount you would save in interest. The calculators at bankrate.com that estimate when debt will be paid off can provide extra incentive. Meanwhile, keeping up with other payments, from utilities to student loans, will protect your credit score from further harm. Bankruptcy, which discharges much of your debts but comes with a steep price, in the form of a ruined credit score for about seven years, is always a last resort.

An even better option would be to avoid that situation in the first place. An emergency fund is usually the first line of protection against such financial catastrophe. When twenty-six-year-old Veronica Neilan, a Brooklyn-based recent graduate with a master's degree in forensic mental health counseling, suddenly needed an emergency root canal, it cost her $1,661—and that was after dental insurance covered its portion. She had to pay for part of it with a health care finance loan from Capital One that came with a twelve-month interest-free period followed by a 20 percent interest rate—a situation that an emergency fund would have prevented. (Even without the emergency fund, she managed to pay off the loan before the interest rate kicked in, which saved her money.)

A root canal, while painful, is nothing compared to more tragic emergencies that require immediate funding. A 2009 survey found that most people don't have enough money socked away to adequately cushion themselves from unexpected divorce, illness, or job loss. Nine in ten said job loss had had a significant negative impact on their finances, as did two-thirds of those who had gone through a divorce.[8]

When you need money fast, depending on financial institutions to give it to you can make you feel even more vulnerable than you already do. That's one reason why Veronica says that even after she gets a job she's going to continue her frugal habits from graduate school and save as much money as she can—along with repaying the $113,000 in student loans she's taken out over the last seven years.

Exercises: Do You Have the Right Amount of Debt?

I. Calculate how much your debt is costing you. What else could you be doing with that money?

	MY TOTAL DEBT	INTEREST RATE	COST PER YEAR (Multiply debt by interest rate.)
Student Loans			
Car Loans			
Credit Cards			
Other			

2. Get a better deal from your credit card company. If you carry any debt on your credit card, then make sure you're minimizing interest payments by negotiating as low an annual rate as possible. Check out the average rates at indexcreditcards.com and see how yours compares. If it's above average, then call your company and ask for a lower one. If you're a good customer with a strong credit score and history of making on-time payments, you have a decent chance of getting it.

3. Make a plan for paying off debt. Do you want to get rid of the high-interest student loan debt within the next five years, instead of maxing out your 401(k) contributions? If you have fast-approaching spending goals such as buying a house, do you want to save money for a down payment before paying off low-interest debt, such as federal student loans?

4. Imagine what being debt free would feel like. If you had no student loan payment to make each month, what would you do with that money? If it would significantly change your life or let you do something that is important to you, then it may be time to dedicate the next six months to living so frugally that you're able to cross that debt off your balance sheet.

5. Give yourself a stress test. How vulnerable are you to sudden job loss or unexpected expenses? Do you have an emergency fund? If not, start building one.

4

INVESTING FOR SMARTIES

Just as deodorant companies sell products by making us paranoid about our bodily odors, the financial services industry thrives on making us feel stupid about money. As long as investing seems complicated and intimidating, we'll continue to pay hefty fees in exchange for someone else's expertise. The financial crisis of 2008 and 2009 helped explode that myth, after even the "experts" were unsuccessful when it came to protecting people's money. It convinced more people of what some of the most skilled investors knew all along: to trust yourself, and only yourself. By following a few basic investing rules, you'll be poised to be as successful as Warren Buffett (albeit on a smaller scale, alas).

In this chapter, you'll learn the following lessons:

1. The investing rules that the gurus live by—and the myths they reject

2. How to select the right risk level, depending on your investment goals

3. How the rules have changed in our post-tech-bubble, post-recession world

GETTING STARTED

After years of spending close to (or more than) what we earn, it's exhilarating to graduate to a stage where we finally have some money to invest. But even though some of the most basic rules of investing have been drilled into us since high school, it's not always easy to follow them.

Consider what happened to J. D. Roth, forty-one, the Portland-based blogger behind the popular personal finance site getrichslowly .org. In his eagerness to grow his Roth IRA account, he invested a year's worth of contributions—around $3,500—in Sharper Image in 2007. If you are at all familiar with the plight of that high-end gadget company, then you may know that his investment was pretty much akin to lighting a pile of bills worth $3,500 on fire.

Why did J. D., whom some consider a god of personal finance, make such a seemingly stupid move? As he readily admits, even though he writes about money, he's just an average guy who makes mistakes and tries to learn from them. Most of his retirement savings are in index funds, after all. But back in 2007, he was talking to a friend who worked at Sharper Image, and that friend told him that he had recently invested in the company himself, which gave J. D. the impression that the share prices were significantly undervalued. So J. D. went for it. And he lost—big time. As J. D. says, "All I was doing was gambling, plain and simple."

J. D. is hardly the only one to be drawn to individual stocks that come with big risks. In fact, it's something many beginning investors do because, let's face it, it's a lot sexier to invest in the company that makes your favorite brand of sneaker, or car, than it is to put your money into the amorphous blob that is "the market." When Jason Barnette, a twenty-nine-year-old software developer in Arlington, Virginia, first started investing in his early twenties, he put about 75 percent of his money into individual stocks, each of which he took time to research, from Intel to Motorola to retail companies. But now, he's shifted half of his investments into index funds while still keeping half in stocks. "I think over time you realize you're less likely to beat the market, and you recognize the index fund approach is better than speculating," he says. Today, even when he wants to focus on specific growth areas, such as China and India, he chooses funds that contain a range of stocks from those countries, instead of just picking one or two.

That's not to say picking individual stocks is a horrible idea for everyone. Sean Hannon, thirty-five-year-old father of four, thrives on it. After he paid off his student loan debt in his mid-twenties, he dedicated the $1,500 a month that had been going toward those payments to the stock market. He first put his money into stocks like Amazon, which were in the midst of the Internet bubble roller coaster. After losing around $10,000 with that strategy, he switched to a more studied one: he started looking for big household-name companies, such as Philip Morris and McDonalds, and researched everything he could about them. He read their financial statements, kept up with their financial news, and even did some calculations to estimate what he thought their stock should be worth. When it was higher than the actual trading price, he would make purchases and then sell the shares as soon as they reached the price he calculated to be fair. Sometimes it would take a week, and other times he would wait for a year or longer. His strategy paid off: his Philip Morris shares, which he had bought for around $15, went up to $70 within two years. He admits he got a bit lucky with his timing, since he was getting into investing around 2000, when many big-name stocks were undervalued.

Soon, friends started asking Sean for help, and after years of working for Deloitte and Goldman Sachs, he formed his own investment firm, Epic Advisors. Based in Westfield, New Jersey, it now manages $25 million in assets. While Sean sticks mostly to his original strategy, he recommends that his clients who have trouble stomaching the ups and downs of individual stocks focus on index funds instead. "If you can't take the volatility and stress, then index funds are probably best," he says.

If you enjoy checking up on your accounts regularly and plugging numbers into spreadsheets, then you can probably handle your own money management. Some people, though, prefer to turn to professionals. If you decide to go that route, make sure to ask potential advisers about their style, credentials, fee structure, and experience before picking one. Consider fee-only advisers, who typically charge between $90 and $300 per hour depending on the region and their level of experience, so they don't have an incentive to push you toward buying and selling certain funds. (Some advisers work for a flat fee or a percentage of the assets being managed.) The websites of the National Association of Personal Financial Advisors (napfa .org) and the Financial Planning Association (fpanet.org) can help you find the right person.

As J. D.'s, Jason's, and Sean's experiences begin to illustrate, there are five basic principles of investing that apply in almost all situations:

1. Diversify investments to minimize your exposure to risk.

2. Start early to maximize the power of compound interest.

3. Pay as little in expenses as possible.

4. Realize that it's impossible to time the market.

5. Accept that higher rewards come with higher risks.

First, the golden rule of diversity: for most people, investing in individual stocks is too risky. Diversification—in stocks, market segments, and specific companies—reduces your chances of losing everything. One of the easiest ways to do that while investing in the stock market is through index funds, which mirror a specific market index such as the S&P 500. Because they are passively managed, meaning they don't rely on a person researching and selecting stocks, they also tend to come with lower fees. Since index funds typically track a broad segment of the market, it doesn't much matter if one company takes a nosedive in the face of the scandal of the century, because the vast majority of your money is elsewhere. Most of the victims of the Bernie Madoff scam suffered particularly bad fates because they had entrusted their entire nest eggs to a man who turned out to be orchestrating a Ponzi scheme (where old investors are paid from new investors' money, not from any actual earnings). Many Enron employees, who had invested much of their savings in Enron stock, faced the same problem when their company collapsed.

The second principle, the power of compounding, is a favorite of high school teachers. It's mouthwatering to see just how quickly interest can build on principal when it compounds regularly. An initial investment of $10,000 more than quadruples to over $43,000 after thirty years at a 5 percent interest rate; at 10 percent, it turns into almost $174,500. That's why saving and investing early works to our advantage. If you put $1,000 into an account that earned 5 percent returns when you were twenty, you'd have around $26,500 by your fortieth birthday. If you waited until age thirty, you'd have just $16,289.

☑ Quick Tip: Buying and Selling Online

Online brokerage companies such as E*Trade and Scottrade make it easy to set up an account and buy and sell stocks from home. While most investors are better off sticking to index and other broad-spectrum funds, some people, like Jason Barnette, find picking stocks to be a really fun hobby. It's a little like golf—time consuming and potentially pricey. In addition to the fees associated with buying and selling stocks, owning individual companies' stocks also puts you at risk for big swings resulting from company or industry news. But if you find the ride enjoyable—and according to a recent Scottrade survey, one in three twenty-something investors say they invest because it's fun[1]—then it might be worth that risk to you, especially if you limit yourself to playing with a relatively small portion of your overall savings.

Third, expenses can pile up like a week's load of dirty laundry, so you want to minimize them as much as possible. While actively managed mutual funds, which rely on a manager to research and pick specific stocks, tend to be more expensive than passively managed index funds, fees for both types of funds vary widely. Generally, they range from 0.1 to 2 percent of the amount that's invested. The think tank RAND calculates that even just one percentage point difference in annual fees adds up to $3,380 after ten years on a $20,000 account balance.[2] But most of us pay up without even realizing it, perhaps because the fee details are often hard to find. (They should be in the fund's prospectus; ask the fund company directly if it's not clear.) RAND found that when people were presented with various fund options, including one that clearly came with the lowest fees, only half of them selected that lowest-fee fund. One in three people inexplicably selected the fund with the highest fees. (All of the funds exhibited equivalent returns.) Because they automatically reduce investor returns, high fees are a primary reason research suggests passively managed index funds perform better for investors than do actively managed mutual funds.

Fourth, no one can time the market. Doing so would require a *Back to the Future*–style time machine. That's where "dollar-cost averaging" comes in. It means investing a little bit at a time, without regard to what the market is doing. For example, say you have $10,000 that you want to put into the stock market over the next couple of years. Instead of putting it all in today, when it could lose half of its value overnight, you would put in $500 a month over twenty months, which makes you less vulnerable to the peaks and troughs of the market. (Of course, you also want to pay attention to the fees involved each time you buy securities, but the benefits of spreading out your purchases will probably outweigh the costs of one-time fees.)

☑ Quick Tip: Know Your (Hormonal) Weakness

Research shows that, in general, men tend to be overly aggressive with their investments, while women tend to be too conservative. Research from the University of Chicago and Northwestern University suggests that testosterone explains the gender difference.[3] Women with high levels of testosterone, as measured through saliva, are more likely to take bigger risks. Make sure your investment choices reflect the amount of risk that makes sense for you, and that they're not overly influenced by hormones.

The last principle, which stipulates that risk increases with reward and vice versa, is not quite as well known. Basically, you can't cheat reality: if an investment comes with a high potential reward, then it also comes with high potential risk—another reason Madoff's investors should have been suspicious when he promised them such high returns with so little apparent risk.

☑ Quick Tip: Choosing a Bank

When deciding on the financial institution that you'll be using to make deposits, withdraw cash, write checks, and take care of most of your other banking needs, the first question you should ask is whether the bank is FDIC insured. If it is, then the money is insured by the federal government for up to $250,000 per account, at least through the end of 2013, when the limit may change. Most banks are FDIC insured. Your next priority is to earn as high a rate of return as possible on savings accounts. Online-only banks, such as ING, tend to offer higher rates of return because they have lower overhead costs. It's easy to do quick comparisons at websites such as bankrate.com.

PICKING TIME HORIZONS

Where you should put your money depends largely on when you plan to spend it, since the farther into the future you will need it, the greater risk you can afford to take. That's why most of a young professional's retirement money belongs in the stock market. But savings earmarked for a home, a teen's college tuition, or emergencies go in safer spots, such as a money market or bond fund. Investment manager Sean Hannon, for example, keeps at least six months of living expenses out of the stock market altogether. He maintains about a month's worth of expenses in his checking account, then funds for months two and three in a savings account that pays a relatively low interest rate, and months four, five, and six in certificates of deposit (or CDs, which are fixed-term deposits that usually come with a slightly higher interest rate than savings accounts).

TYPE OF SAVINGS VEHICLE	EXPECTED RETURN	BEST IF YOU NEED MONEY
Checking accounts	Usually 0 percent	Immediately
Savings accounts	0 to 2 percent	0 to 6 months
Certificate of deposit	0.5 to 3 percent	6 months to 5 years
Money market fund	0.5 to 4 percent	0 to 5 years
Bond fund	3 to 10 percent	1 to 10 years
Stock market	-10 to 10 percent	10 to 60 years

Money market funds, which invest in short-term, low-risk securities, are like homemade spaghetti sauce—a great, comfortable alternative to the default savings account that usually pays a return below the rate of inflation. Money market funds generally pay a higher return, but you can still withdraw the money almost immediately. (In times of higher uncertainty, such as during recessions, more people tend to put their money in these safe spots, so the yields can drop significantly, sometimes close to zero, because there is so much money out there competing for those safe returns.) In general, they carry little risk (although during the credit crisis of 2008 at least one fund lost money). Tax-exempt money market funds, which usually carry a lower rate of return but let investors avoid federal, and sometimes state, taxes because they invest in municipal securities, are a good option for people in high tax brackets. All those traits make money market funds the go-to place for short-term savings. Over the long term, though, inflation can eat away at those returns. Bond funds that invest in longer-term debt, such as corporate bonds, carry greater risk but also pay higher rates of return. If you're willing to stomach a bit more volatility, they can pay off.

☑ Quick Tip: Investing Resources

For up-to-date news on stocks, companies, and the economy:
- finance.yahoo.com
- google.com/finance

For lessons from other young investors:
- stocktradingtogo.com

For tips from the experts:
- *The Little Book of Common Sense Investing* by John C. Bogle
- *A Random Walk Down Wall Street* by Burton Malkiel
- *The Four Pillars of Investing* by William Bernstein

For Kenneth and Danielle, our typical young professional couple, most of their savings, other than their retirement accounts, are for short-term goals—emergencies and their first home. As a result, they don't put any of it in the stock market. Instead, they put half of their now-significant sum (after two years of marriage, they've saved $50,000) into a tax-exempt money market fund and half into a slightly riskier but higher-earning corporate bond fund. On the former, they earn a 4 percent return, which nets them $1,000 a year; on the latter, they earn a 6 percent return, which brings in $1,500 a year. That means they get an additional $2,500 of income a year just by managing their savings well.

THE 1990s ARE OVER, AND THEY'RE NOT COMING BACK

That's good news for those of us who were never fans of the grunge look, but bad news for anyone hoping to earn 10 percent returns every year. Books, magazines, and other sources of personal finance expertise continue to push the notion that we shouldn't worry about the fact that, after we factor in the recent down market, the stock market has returned next to nothing over the past ten years. On average, these stock market cheerleaders say, returns have always historically returned around 10 percent a year.[4]

But it's very possible—probable, some might say—that they are wrong, and that 10 percent average returns were an anomaly unique to the twentieth century. Since 2000, returns have been significantly lower. Some prominent sources, including the *Economist* and *Wall Street Journal*, have even referred to the 2000s as a "lost decade" for investors.[5] Anyone trying to estimate their returns for the next few decades might want to consider using a more conservative estimate of 6 or 8 percent returns, and even that feels a bit optimistic. After all, Japan's stock market is still struggling to return to levels it experienced two decades ago.

But rather than wallowing in potential doomsday scenarios or lamenting how unlucky our generation is that the stock market started sinking as soon as we began investing in it, we can consider ourselves fortunate that the crash of 2008 didn't come later, when we were closer to retirement. Or we can simply be grateful that it happened. As Suze Orman has pointed out, if the economy had kept on going the way it did in the 1990s, we would still be buying expensive stocks and overinflated real estate. The financial crisis, she says, is the greatest thing that has ever happened to our generation. (Suze, of course, says this with the knowledge that most of her money is safely ensconced in bond funds.) People who are just starting to invest have had a unique opportunity to buy into the stock market at the lowest prices in years. And plenty of experts are quick to point to the data on historical returns, which suggest that there's no way we could possibly have two "lost decades" in a row, and market returns will surely rebound back to twentieth-century levels before too long.

Meanwhile, we can take steps to make the most of the post–credit crunch markets, starting with these pieces of advice:

- **Accept reality.** The heyday of easy returns and overnight millionaires is probably over, at least for now. We can't count on the stock market returning to 10 percent returns anytime soon. That means you'll need to save more to achieve the same long-term wealth goals.

- **But don't give up on the market.** It still offers the potential of steep rewards. Selling stocks after the market has plunged only guarantees you one thing: losses. As long as your investments are well diversified (index funds and mutual funds that are exposed to a broad range of sectors) and age appropriate (more aggressive when younger, more conservative when older), then you should just sit back, relax, and try to think about something other than the stock market.

- **When the market drops, rebalance your accounts.** Dramatic losses often mean you have a greater percentage of your money in safer investments, such as bonds, and a smaller percentage in more aggressive, longer-term stocks, since your stocks have lost so much value. For example, if you had half of your savings in stocks and half in bonds, after the market plummeted you would suddenly have most of your money in bonds. Rebalancing can mean buying into a weak stock market, which goes against instinct, but it's often a winning strategy. Research suggests that investors often fail to make these adjustments, which costs them in the long run. One ING DIRECT study found that two in three Americans made no adjustments to their investments in the wake of the most recent recession.[7]

- **Learn from your mistakes.** After J. D. Roth had his Sharper Image fiasco, he decided to focus exclusively on index funds, including bond, stock, and real estate funds. Through a Fidelity index fund that invests in the S&P 500 as well as international stocks, he's now exposed to a broad swath of the market.

If you need to cheer yourself up when your investments are suffering, try these strategies:

- **Plan an evening at home.** Whether you enjoy cooking, watching movies, or playing video games on your couch, staying home is a good way to have fun without spending much money. It can also provide a sense of stability during market volatility.
- **Adopt a new (inexpensive) hobby.** Long bike rides, knitting, and grilling a great steak don't take much cash, and the Internet can offer lessons on any technical skills you need. (Just search youtube.com or wikihow.com for how-to videos or articles on the skill you want to learn.)
- **Focus on people.** Arranging to spend an afternoon with a friend, your spouse, or your mom won't cost more than $10, even if it includes a stop at a coffee shop.
- **Avoid cable television news.** Twenty-four hours a day, the financial news channels analyze every dip and peak of the market. As a result, watching them can make even a relatively calm day seem as if it's filled with drama. The national evening news, on the other hand, can be quite soothing—whether you prefer the calm and authoritative tones of Brian Williams or Katie Couric, their consistency can be as relaxing as a long walk on the beach. For some of us.

Even after studying these investing strategies, most of us are pretty much destined to make mistakes, especially at first. That's another reason to start investing as soon as possible. Even though J. D., Sean, and Jason took some hits investing at an early age, they also learned lessons that could otherwise have taken a lifetime. If J. D. had invested in a company on the brink of bankruptcy at age sixty, it would have been much more harmful to his portfolio. As painful as it is, losing money can be the best motivator for sticking with the basic, time-tested investing principles going forward.

Exercises: What's Your Investment Strategy Doing for You?

1. Make a list of all of your savings and investment accounts. Include the amount in each one, interest being earned, and the approximate year you might want that money. Is the money that you don't need for a while earning as much interest as it could be? Or is money you plan to use soon at risk? Rebalance your accounts so they reflect those goals.

2. Consider whether your investments follow the basic rules of investing. Are they diversified? Are you starting to invest as soon as possible to take advantage of compounding? Are you minimizing your fees?

3. Check up on your investment accounts and see what the expenses are. If you have money in funds that are charging you over 1 percent of assets each year, consider moving it to a cheaper option.

4. Decide if you want to work with a personal finance adviser. If you do decide to hire one, look for a fee-only adviser to avoid conflicts of interest. If your company offers free 401(k) financial adviser services, take advantage of that opportunity.

5. Try to ignore the daily fluctuations of long-term investments. If a bad day in the market makes for a stressful evening, consider checking on your investments just once a month and ignoring them the rest of the time, or putting your funds in a safer place.

5

NOT YOUR PARENTS' RETIREMENT

While many of us dream of a cushy double-decade retirement, we aren't always saving enough to prepare for it. We don't have pensions, the Social Security trust fund is set to run out of money just as we retire, and our 401(k)s haven't exactly been earning impressive returns. That's why we need to save much more than any standard financial calculator would typically recommend, plan on funding our retirements almost entirely with our own savings and investments, and start as soon as possible, even if we're only saving $25 a month at first.

In this chapter, you'll learn the following:

1. Why our retirement years will look nothing like our parents' (and even less like our grandparents')

2. How to figure out just how much money you'll need in your dotage (a lot)

3. How to start saving toward a million-dollar-plus retirement fund

REALITY BITES

On an early summer day in 2009 in the Rayburn House Office Building on Capitol Hill, the marble hallways lack the normal clickety-clack of high heels, the security lines haven't yet formed, and the basement deli is empty. But the chatter of twenty-somethings livens up the end of one hallway. By 8:30 a.m., an hour before most official Hill business gets under way, a group of about thirty has gathered for the 2009 Youth Entitlements Summit to discuss the future of Social Security and Medicare. As the participants file in, they greet each other and catch up. It feels a bit like happy hour, but with coffee instead of booze.

Twenty-four-year-old Thierry Dongala, the master of ceremonies for the day and vice president of the youth advocacy group Americans for Generational Equity, calls the meeting to order. He looks a lot like Dulé Hill, the actor who played the personal aide to President Bartlet on *The West Wing*, and he shares that character's earnestness as well. Thierry introduces Representative John C. Spratt, a Democratic congressman from South Carolina and chairman of the House Budget Committee, who warns the group of the looming deficits that lie ahead. The elder statesman stands in sharp contrast to the optimistic youth in his audience, and he doesn't want to leave them with the impression that any of this is going to be easy. "We could be heading into a Japanese-like recovery, which is weak and slow," he says.

A group of three economists speak next, each with a warning more dire than the next. The speaker from the conservative CATO Institute says that the government makes entitlement benefits seem more stable than they are to stave off concern, but that leads young people to save less money than they should. He urges his audience to vote in elections, keeping their economic interests primary in their minds. The health care expert from the liberal-leaning Brookings Institution says the recent financial crisis has only proven that Social Security must remain strong and secure, since other savings and investments can't always be counted on.

To underscore the seriousness of the topic, twenty-eight-year-old Kouri Marshall, the youth leader charged with moderating the economists' debate, warns the group that "inaction will lead to our certain demise," given the anticipated shortfalls in the Social Security trust fund well before his generation retires. He calls on Travis Johnson, representative for the Young Democrats of Louisiana, who asks the economists to explain just how bad things are going to get.

The answer, from Jagadeesh Gokhale, the CATO economist, is that they will get very, very bad. Imagine, he explains, that you are circling around a vortex. All seems calm, as it might to you right now. But eventually you will be trapped at the bottom, your juices will be sucked out, and "you'll be spit out." The crowd laughs nervously.

Jagadeesh's metaphor, though, is not that far off from the warnings of other experts. The Social Security trust fund will start taking in less than it pays out around 2016, and by 2037, as today's thirty-somethings start thinking about retiring, it's scheduled to run out.[1] At that point, if nothing changes, the benefits will shrink to about three-quarters of what they are now because only money that is then being paid into the system will be paid out. That has led to a debate over whether the current budget and entitlement structure is fair to young people, who may never see the money that they pay into the system. (Social Security benefits are based on a person's average earnings over his lifetime and depend on the age of retirement; the current maximum benefit received is $2,346 per month for those who retire at age sixty-six.[2])

"They should be upset, and concerned that Social Security is structured in a way to give them less than they might otherwise receive. They'll certainly get less than their parents and grandparents, and they're stuck in a position where they are either going to pay higher taxes or get lower benefits, or, what's worse, both," says David John, senior fellow at the Heritage Foundation.

But when I ask the AARP, which represents retired Americans, whether this system, which might only be able to pay out 75 cents on the dollar when today's young workers get ready to collect their checks, is fair, the response is dismissive. "I've never heard people talk about it that way," says Cristina Martin Firvida, the AARP's director of economic security. "Everyone knows and agrees that will not come to pass. We won't come to a point where we're going to let the program slide," she says.

Her response illustrates much of the intergenerational divide. "The AARP sometimes acts resentful when young people get worked up. But it's true. There's no way Social Security is as good a deal for a twenty-year-old as it is for a retiree today," says Andrew Biggs of the American Enterprise Institute. Laurence Kotlikoff, author of *The Coming Generational Storm* and a longtime advocate of reform, is even blunter. He calls Social Security a "Ponzi scheme" that victimizes our generation.

Back at the youth summit, the participants are ready to break for lunch with David Walker, a celebrity in the world of federal budgeting. He served as comptroller general under presidents Clinton and George W. Bush and now leads the Peter G. Peterson Foundation, where he continues to warn of the dangers of overspending and a growing federal budget. David Walker tells me later that he doesn't ascribe to the part of the debate that stokes a sense of conflict between the generations. He explains that Social Security was never designed to be a quid pro quo system, but rather to provide extra income to lower-income groups at the expense of those with higher incomes, in order to alleviate financial hardship among the elderly. "I hear young people saying, 'I'm not getting a good deal.' That's technically right, but it doesn't reflect the nature of what Social Security is," he says.

Still, it's hard to ignore the fact that we're inheriting such a different arrangement from the one offered to our parents and grandparents. In our parents' day, companies were much more likely to offer pension plans with guaranteed payouts in retirement. Social Security looked as stable as the love between Paul Newman and Joanne Woodward. Lazy retirements filled with sunny days at the beach and yacht club dinners loomed in the future. Now, not only is the future of Social Security uncertain, but we're lucky if our company provides us with a 401(k) plan that allows us to take our chances in the stock market. Guaranteed pensions aren't even on the table.

But the AARP is right to point out that a lot could change over our working lifetimes. For starters, Social Security could be overhauled so benefits don't end up drying up, but that would probably mean higher payroll taxes, most likely for those who earn over $106,800, which is the current income cap on Social Security taxes. (If you make more than that, then you've probably noticed that your paychecks suddenly get higher whenever your income reaches that limit each year.) The retirement age could also go from sixty-five to sixty-eight, instead of the sixty-seven it's currently scheduled to reach, or the cost-of-living benefit increases could be reduced. One set of changes costs us more, and the other pays us less. (Another unknown is the future of Medicare, which is also funded in part by payroll taxes. If premiums or Medicare-related taxes are increased or benefits are reduced, that would also have a major negative impact on our generation's retirement finances.)

Some academics urge out-of-the-box changes. Alicia Munnell, director of Boston College's Center for Retirement Research, has proposed a new kind of "guaranteed" retirement savings account where the government absorbs much of the risk.[3] That way, if the market experiences big downturns just as people are getting ready to retire, they don't suffer the fate of the current slew of retirees. She imagines the government offering a modest guaranteed rate of return on these accounts, such as 6 percent. If the rate of return is lower than that, then Uncle Sam would make up the difference. Since she calculates, based on historical returns, that the government would rarely have to step in, the costs of such a program would be minimal, she says. It would be expensive in periods such as the current one, but Professor Munnell says the government can absorb that kind of risk, since it can spread out the cost over several generations. (Of course, the younger generations called on to pony up that money for current retirees might have a different opinion, as the Youth Entitlement Summit demonstrates.)

Right now, though, such major changes are still in the distant future. And while a new savings program might come along or Congress might reform Social Security, the benefits are unlikely to be targeted at relatively high-earning young professionals, who are deemed capable of taking care of themselves. So we have to make sure we're doing just that. Many of us are already planning to do so: a Charles Schwab survey found that members of Generation Y, who are now mostly in their twenties, estimate that 61 percent of their money in retirement will come from their personal savings and investments.[4] That's 20 percentage points higher than the estimate given by baby boomers, who plan to rely more on Social Security and pensions.

WHY A MILLION ISN'T ANYWHERE CLOSE TO ENOUGH

So how large should those personal coffers be? A million dollars might sound like the ticket to a beachfront resort near West Palm Beach, with an endless supply of gin and tonics, but a tiny apartment in downtown Miami with cans of Bud Light is more like it. It would provide $50,000 worth of income for about twenty years (assuming the money earns a 5 percent return throughout retirement and after adjusting for taxes and inflation), which means you could pretty much count on being poverty-stricken in your eighties.[5]

For someone like our friend Kenneth, who now earns $90,000 in his early thirties, a more realistic goal to aim for is around $2 to $3 million, which, depending on inflation and interest rates, would likely comfortably replace his income from ages sixty-five through ninety-five. But the only way to know how much you really need is to do the math yourself with an online calculator. Your financial institution might offer a personalized one; Fidelity, T. D. Ameritrade, Transamerica, and T. Rowe Price are among those that do. Whichever calculator you use, be sure to experiment with a variety of unknowns, including inflation, rate of return, tax rate, and length of retirement.

The vast majority of people—nine in ten—never calculate how much money they need to save for retirement.[6] That could explain why, on average, we're on track to replace less than 60 percent of our incomes once we retire. But financial advisers recommend that we replace at least 80 percent of our former salaries, considering the rising cost of health care. According to the Employee Benefit Research Institute, the average employee contributes just 7.5 percent of his earnings into his 401(k) account.[7] Experts say the number should be closer to 15 percent in order to build up enough money over the decades.[8]

After the dramatic stock market losses of 2008 and early 2009, I crunched some numbers of my own, using a free online calculator on bankrate.com. I had long assumed that I was saving plenty (around 10 percent of my annual income since I started working in my early twenties). But the calculator told me that at my current savings rate I'd be able to support myself for only eleven years. I've since made some adjustments and started contributing close to the maximum allowed, currently around $16,000 a year.

✅ Quick Tip: 401(k)s and Beyond

Here's a brief overview of common retirement savings vehicles:
- **401(k):** The most popular tool for retirement savings is offered through employers, who often match a certain percentage of contributions. (Public school employees have access to the equivalent, 403(b)s.) The money is deposited and grows tax free, but you'll pay taxes when you make withdrawals. Companies, though, are under no legal obligation to continue

providing matches, and they often drop them during tough times. One survey found that during the most recent recession one in five employers reduced their 401(k) matching programs.[9] If you leave your job, you can roll over your 401(k) into either an IRA account or your new company's 401(k) plan to avoid any early withdrawal fees and continue to delay paying taxes on the money. (Some companies allow former employees to leave the money in their 401(k)s indefinitely. If you are happy with the investment choices and don't mind managing multiple accounts, then that might be a good option, especially if you have frequently switched jobs since entering the workforce or are now self-employed.)

- **Roth IRA:** You deposit money into this account after paying taxes on it, but when you withdraw the money it's tax free. Because of relatively low maximum annual contribution levels and income limits, this account generally makes sense for people who are earning low- to mid-level incomes, such as students and entry-level employees. If your tax rate is lower now than it will be when you take the money out, you'll benefit.

- **Traditional IRA:** Contributions are tax deductible, but taxes are paid upon withdrawal. Like the Roth IRA, strict income limits render this vehicle unavailable to many young professionals, but it can be useful during periods of low income.

- **Roth 401(k):** This relatively new savings account, introduced in 2006, allows workers to invest post-tax dollars into an account that is protected from future taxes. In general, it works best for two types of people: those who have already built up a large balance in their existing, pre-tax 401(k)s and want to diversify their investments so they are not all subject to the same tax treatment, and those who are earning less now than they expect to in the future (since they're in a lower tax bracket). Not all employers offer the Roth 401(k), so you might have to ask your human resources manager about it.

There are no limits on how much money you can save, just on how much you can put into tax-shielded accounts. So if you have extra retirement savings after contributing the annual maximum to your 401(k), consider funneling that money into a post-tax account such as an ordinary savings or investment account, where you can invest in stock and bond funds. If you're on the other extreme, and going through a period of lower earnings (and lower savings), then consider a Roth IRA. Your income might be low enough to qualify, and you won't miss out on any market growth during those years. If your paycheck has disappeared because you're taking care of kids, then you might qualify for a spousal IRA, which is for nonworking spouses. A portion of the working spouse's income can be directed into an IRA for the stay-at-home spouse.

☑ Quick Tip: The Tax Factor

When you're making your retirement savings calculations, don't forget to factor in taxes. According to the University of Michigan Retirement Research Center, married college graduates, who tend to be otherwise well-prepared for retirement, falter when it comes to anticipating exactly what they'll owe Uncle Sam. The percentage of those who are prepared for retirement falls to 74 percent from 92 percent after taxes are taken into account.[10] Many online retirement calculators incorporate tax estimates; make sure yours does.

When it comes to choosing which funds to invest in, the same basic investing principles apply: the longer you have until retirement, the more aggressive you want your investments to be. Typically, people in their twenties should have 80 to 100 percent of their retirement savings in stock funds. Since index funds that mirror market indexes such as the S&P 500 usually come with the lowest expense ratios, those should be the top choice. People in their thirties need to be a bit more conservative, with 20 to 40 percent of their money in bond funds and the rest in stocks. The older one gets, the more conservative one should become. A standard rule of thumb is to subtract your age from 100, or, to be more aggressive, from 110. That's the percentage you should have in stocks; the rest should be in bonds and other safer vehicles. Unfortunately, many people make the mistake of investing too conservatively when they're young and too aggressively when they're older.

According to Vanguard founder John Bogle, almost two in ten twenty-something investors own no stocks whatsoever. Instead, they're in much lower-risk, lower-return vehicles such as money market funds and stable value funds.[11] There's not much chance that those accounts will keep up with inflation, which makes them just slightly more useful than stashing the money in a freezer.

Some mutual funds, known as life-cycle or target-date funds, make those shifts for you as you age, but they often come with high expenses. In fact, you want to be sure to check up on all of the fees associated with your retirement accounts, since they add up over the decades. According to Bogle, the average stock fund has an expense ratio of around 1.3 percent, which excludes transaction costs incurred when specific stocks are bought and sold. If you include those costs as well, then, he estimates, expenses range from 1.5 percent to 2.3 percent a year. Those expenses could easily eat up half of the returns of a fund that pays 4 percent a year. Over fifty years, he calculates, those expenses consume almost three-quarters of the wealth that has accumulated.[12]

Q. I've been saving up for retirement in my 401(k), but now I want to go back to school to get my MBA. Can I use that money to pay for it?

A. Probably not, at least not without paying a 10 percent penalty on the amount withdrawn. While there are some exceptions to the rules about early withdrawals, including for "hardship" situations, going to business school would not likely qualify. If your plan allows it, you could potentially take out a loan against the 401(k) account, but then you'll miss out on any market growth during those years and be on the hook to repay it. Since you know you're going back to school, you should instead direct your post-tax savings into a 529 plan, which is a tax-sheltered account dedicated to education costs. In most cases, it can be used to pay for graduate school. That way, you'll avoid paying taxes on gains and a withdrawal penalty. (Money in IRAs can also be put toward educational expenses without being subject to the 10 percent penalty, although you might have to pay income tax on the amount withdrawn.)

The no-timing-the-market principle also applies here. While some research has suggested that significant gains happen on a relatively small percentage of trading days, anticipating those days is pretty much impossible.[13] That's why dollar-cost averaging, which happens automatically with paycheck 401(k) deductions, is your best bet. In fact, when your money is invested through your paycheck, you can't even tell when, exactly, it's buying shares. The investment involves a two-step process: First, your company sends your contribution to the financial institution that's doing the investing. (Fidelity is the country's largest plan administrator.) Even though it sounds simple, this step doesn't necessarily happen on payday itself; there can be a delay of a day or more. Second, the plan administrator takes the money and invests it at the next available "net asset value" of the fund, which is usually determined at 4 p.m. Eastern time each day, at the close of the market.

☑ Quick Tip: A Warning for the Single Ladies

Research from the Transamerica Center for Retirement shows that many single women aren't saving anywhere close to what they need for retirement. On average, the center estimates that a single woman needs to have saved $500,000 by the time she retires. (For the reasons explained previously, that's a relatively conservative estimate, and probably far too little for a young professional who wants to replenish her income without relying on government entitlement programs or company pensions.) But according to its annual survey, most are on track to store up much less than that. One-third of single female respondents have saved less than $25,000 and only one in ten have saved more than $100,000. Only 6 percent have calculated how much they will need to fund their lifestyle once they stop working.[14] In general, women need to save more than men because they are more likely to live longer. For more information, visit the Women's Institute for a Secure Retirement at wiserwomen.org.

BABY STEPS

In her mid-twenties, Nicole Mladic, a public relations executive in Chicago, was living paycheck to paycheck on the equivalent of a teacher's salary. When one of her paychecks was delayed in December 2004, she was almost forced to skip Christmas presents and New Year's celebrations. She didn't even bother opening a 401(k) because the standard recommendation seemed impossible. "I thought I could never put away 10 percent [of my income], so I wasn't putting away anything," recalls Nicole, now thirty-one.

So the energetic fashionista, who writes about her spending habits on her Budgeting Babe blog, started slowly. To free up extra cash, she started comparison shopping online (including on eBay) and not letting herself buy items that weren't on her list when she was out at stores. She also shared her savings goals with her friends, so they wouldn't push her to go to expensive concerts or on pricey trips to Las Vegas. "I can't achieve my goals if my friends aren't aware I'm working toward them," she says. Since they did know about them, they understood when she said she needed a cheap night in instead of going out to a bar. Writing about her progress on her blog gave her extra motivation. And each time she met a goal, she rewarded herself with an affordable night out or annual vacation.

Soon, Nicole opened her 401(k) and started contributing 2 percent of her salary. A few months later, she raised it to 3 and then 4 percent, and eventually she was close to her goal of 10 percent. She also opened a savings account, and started putting in $25 each month. A few promotions and raises later, she raised that amount to $1,000 per month. This slow-but-steady approach works for other people, too: a 2009 survey by HSBC Direct found that while just two in ten Americans constantly save, even though they don't have any particular reason to, other people with less ingrained savings habits can teach themselves to be as thrifty, starting by arranging automatic deposits from their paychecks into savings accounts.[15]

GENERATION EARN

Within a few years, Nicole had one easily accessible savings account for emergencies and one for her down payment fund, which she invested in a money market account. Her money now works for her: When she started her savings account, she earned 15 cents in the first month, and now she makes at least $500 in interest each year. Despite the financial crisis and losing 40 percent of her 401(k), her net worth has gone from $2,600 to $82,000 in a little over three years. She's taken savings into her own hands because, like the rest of us, she doesn't know what kind of entitlement programs will be around when she's sixty-five. And she's not counting on any.

Exercises: Are You Saving Enough?

1. Find your most recent statement from the Social Security Administration, which comes once a year. It lists your earnings record and estimates your future benefits. (It also serves as a nice reminder of the progress you've made since that minimum wage job you took at age sixteen.) Before looking at the statement, take a guess. How much do you think you'll receive each month if you stop working at age sixty-two? What about seventy? You might be surprised by what a big difference delaying retirement makes.

2. Use a retirement calculator at bankrate.com to estimate how much money you'll have at retirement, and how long you'll be able to support yourself, based on your current savings rate. If it's not enough for the lifestyle you had in mind, make a plan to start saving more.

3. Do a quick evaluation of your retirement investments by subtracting your age from 100 (or 110, if you prefer a more aggressive strategy). That's roughly the percentage you should have in stocks, while the rest should be in safer vehicles such as bond funds. That means if you're thirty-five, about 65 percent should be in stock funds and 35 percent should be in bond funds.

4. Review your saving tendencies, weaknesses, and lifestyle. Is your income temporarily lower because you're taking time out of the workforce for school or raising children? If so, can you open a Roth IRA or spousal IRA account?

Part 2

CREATING A HOME

6

WHEN PARENTS ARE LANDLORDS (OR TENANTS)

Once upon a time, back when *Sex and the City* was still on the air, living with one's parents as a grown adult was considered embarrassing. But now, young Americans have gone the way of Japanese twenty-somethings and realized the beauty of intergenerational living arrangements. It saves money, allows extended parent-child bonding, lets young people live in houses they probably couldn't afford on their own, and enables their parents to offset their own living expenses. It's a win-win situation.

In this chapter, you'll learn the following:

1. When it makes sense to move in with your parents, or invite them to move in with you

2. When to give financial assistance to family members, or when to accept it from them

3. When and how to formalize those arrangements

BETTER TOGETHER

Keith Hewson, a thirty-one-year-old pilot, never imagined he'd spend the first year of married life living with his in-laws. When he first moved into the three-bedroom Houston townhouse that his wife's parents had purchased as their retirement home, he and his wife, Katy, a thirty-year-old social worker, were the only residents. His in-laws lived 1,400 miles away just outside of Annapolis, Maryland, and the younger couple paid them rent each month just like any other tenant would. Then, Keith's sixty-one-year-old father-in-law, Gary Smith, retired, and he and his wife, Cindy, sixty-two, moved into the townhouse with Keith and Katy.

What sounds like the premise of a tense reality television show turned out to more closely resemble *The Brady Bunch*. Financially, both couples benefited. The Hewsons stopped paying rent but covered all of the utilities, including the cable, gas, and electric bills. The money they had formerly put toward rent could now go into a down payment fund for their first home as well as into paying off credit card and student loan debt. Keith estimates they were able to save close to $1,500 a month as a result. The Smiths, meanwhile, covered the mortgage and saved what they would have otherwise been spending on monthly bills. Katy, who has the same blond hair and wide smile as her mother, worked out the specifics of who'd pay for what with her parents before they all moved in together.

After a year, Keith and Katy's dream of buying a home of their own came true. They used the down payment money they had saved, but they didn't move far. They settled on a three-bedroom house with a yard about seven blocks away from the townhouse. And then they asked the Smiths to move in with them.

Before he and Katy had even discussed it, Keith asked his in-laws if they wanted to rent out the townhouse to new tenants and join him and Katy in the new place. Now, the couples' roles are reversed: the Smiths pay for the groceries, utilities, and other bills while the Hewsons cover the mortgage. Cindy continues to cook dinners and does much of the cleaning around the house, while Gary takes care of outdoor yard work. "I'm the maid, housekeeper, and cook," Cindy jokes. In fact, she often has dinner ready by the time Katy gets home from work.

The financial benefits for both couples also continue: the Smiths recently used the money they had saved over a four-month period—$4,000—to go on a twenty-eight-day cruise to Western Europe, Scandinavia, and the Baltic Sea. They are able to live off of Gary's pension and delay tapping into any savings. "It's been great to keep expenses low until we learn how far the money stretches in retirement," says Cindy. Plus, Cindy adds, she and Gary get access to cable service and an Internet connection, which they probably wouldn't bother paying for on their own. The Smiths also say they're not sure they would have spent the money to live in such a trendy area, close to shopping and restaurants, if they weren't sharing some of the expenses. Meanwhile, the townhouse rental turns a handy $500 profit a month. And with no bills to pay, the Hewsons have an extra $800 or so each month to save or spend.

> ### ☑ Quick Tip: Caring for Dependent Parents
>
> Living together with parents might be more than just a short-term, money-saving strategy. For some families, multigenerational living serves as a longer-term way to care for parents as they age and need increasing amounts of assistance. If you know your parents will need financial help once they retire or become unable to work—and it's never too early to ask them if they think they'll need that kind of help—then you'll need to start planning in advance. If you expect your aging parents to live with you one day, then you might want to consider homes that contain separate quarters, such as an in-law suite or roomy basement, that can function as a rental unit or au pair suite now and a bedroom for parents later. A recent survey by Coldwell Banker Real Estate found that 37 percent of its agents said that their clients were increasingly interested in homes that could house multiple generations.[1]

In addition to setting money aside for your own retirement, you also might want to siphon away cash into a parents' fund that can help cushion the costs of elder care later. It's not easy to prioritize that kind of saving when there's so much competition for your money, but if you know that you will be responsible for funding your parents' future expenses, then putting even $50 a month into a savings account now could relieve a lot of stress later. The most important step you can take today is to sit down and talk with your parents about their own plans and expectations. Do they have money set aside in case they become seriously ill and need full-time care? Do they envision living in a nursing home one day, or do they strongly prefer to live with family (in other words, you)? Talking about the kind of life and health insurance they have and how they would pay for any long-term care needs is also important; the best strategies will vary by family and health situation. These are difficult questions to bring up, but they're essential for making sure you're all on the same page.

It's not just about the money. Keith likes knowing that Katy isn't alone when his pilot job keeps him away for much of the workweek. Katy also is glad to have the time with her parents. "I'm going to be part of the sandwich generation, where I'll be taking care of my kids and elderly parents at some point, so it's good now we're able to be a family—to enjoy them as adults," she says. Cindy agrees, and says she and her daughter have become even closer than they were before. "When Katy comes home from work, we're excited to hear what went on. It's not just chatting on the phone," she says. She's quick to add that the four of them don't stick together every evening. They often go their separate ways after dinner, since the Smiths' bedroom is big enough to serve as a private living room, as well. "We try to stay out of their way. We're trying to behave so they want to keep us around." If Katy and Keith want the house to themselves for the night, Katy just lets her parents know, and they go out. Keith says he doesn't ever want his in-laws to leave, but Katy thinks the house might get a bit crowded as they start a family. However long they continue living together, both couples have already saved tens of thousands of dollars, without feeling like they've made any sacrifices.

Keith thinks the arrangement could work for more families, if they could get past the stigma. "I definitely don't think I'm unique," he says. "It might be more unusual for Americans to live with their family in this day and age, but in other countries, it's totally normal." He's right. In some western European countries, more than half of thirty-year-old men still live with their parents.[2] Meanwhile, a 2010 study from the Pew Research Center found that multigenerational living in the United States is at a fifty-year high, partly because of the down economy. Some 49 million Americans—16 percent of the population—now live in homes containing two or more adult generations.[3]

But in some relationships, financial benefits flow in only one direction. And those can be much more fraught with complications.

☑ Quick Tip: Going Dutch

Before sharing a roof with your parents, talk about how you're each going to benefit. Will one of you pay rent to the other? Will you evenly split up bills and chores? If living together won't work for you or you don't live near family members, consider other types of cost-sharing arrangements, such as offering to make your mom a website for her small business in exchange for her babysitting for you on a few Saturday nights.

BROTHER, CAN YOU SPARE A DIME?

When Tarah, thirty, was growing up, she watched her parents struggle with their finances. They often asked other family members for money, and even Tarah herself, who held a part-time job as a teen. She didn't mind helping to pay for groceries and car insurance, since she was living at their house, but as she got older, her parents' requests got bigger.

Recently, Tarah's parents asked her to help them buy a new car. Tarah and her husband, who have three kids, decided it would put too much strain on their own budget. "I just couldn't do it," says Tarah, who's trained as an insurance saleswoman and lives in the Midwest. Even though she feels a sense of obligation to her parents, with whom she has an otherwise close relationship, she says, "I know that whenever I help them, I'm enabling them to be just as bad [with money] as they've always been." After Tarah turned down their request, her parents managed to find a fifteen-year-old van that someone was giving away for free. Tarah says that their relationship was tense for about a month, but now her parents are supportive of her and her husband's efforts to stay on top of their own finances.

Tarah's situation is increasingly common. Fidelity reports that about one in ten thirty- and forty-somethings provides financial support to their parents or in-laws, and the average amount is around $3,500 a year.[4] As those parents age, the aid will likely expand. A 2008 Charles Schwab survey found that two in five people expect to eventually provide financial support to their parents, and one in four anticipates needing to give money to siblings.[5] (An even greater number of parents give money to their adult children, an equally dicey issue that we'll talk about in a moment.[6])

When your parents need help and you can happily afford it, then providing support can be a wonderful gift. But when it turns into an enabling habit, or strains your own budget, that usually means it's time to establish some boundaries, as Tarah did.

The first step is to set limits on the amount you're able to give, and to talk about them, both with your significant other and needy family members. Instead of responding to financial requests as they come up—when a car breaks down, after a basement floods—consider telling your parents (or siblings) that you are able to give them a certain amount for the entire year. They can use that money however they need it, but there won't be any more of it. That will help them plan their own budget.

Once you hand over a check, the money is out of your control. If your parents end up using it to fund a trip to Australia, there's nothing you can do about it (except decide not to front them any more cash). Because loans often turn into gifts since they never get repaid, outright gifts are usually a better idea. (If you do give a loan, be sure to put the details in writing.) Another option is to offer to pay for a specific expense, such as car payments or health insurance premiums. If you can, try to help the struggling family member regain control of his or her financial life—it will make your life easier, too. Can you identify the problem areas that are causing the person to leak cash? Does he or she need help filing for bankruptcy? Moving into a smaller home? Learning to say no to friends who want to go on expensive vacations?

If you are unable to give as much money as your parents may need or want, look for nonfinancial alternatives. Perhaps you can invite them over for dinner, or even to temporarily live with you. (It could turn out to be mutually beneficial, as it was for the Hewsons and Smiths.)

You might end up deciding that the best choice for you is to be as generous and understanding as possible. Parents facing financial trouble have often just gone through a divorce, the death of a spouse, or unexpected unemployment. And they are at least partially responsible for your own success, after all.

☑ Quick Tip: To Lend or Not to Lend

After I wrote about lending to family members on my Alpha Consumer blog, readers shared these stories about how it worked (or didn't work) for them:

- In 2005, Andrew lent his sister, who was struggling to pay her bills and get out of debt, $10,000, with the expectation that she would pay him back in full. Today, she's paid back only $800 of it. That creates tension at family gatherings, and Andrew isn't sure how to handle the situation. "I rarely talk to her, and when I do, I don't want to pester her about the money. She recently purchased a house, and she has a family with three stepkids and one child of her own who is only a year old," he says.

- At age fifty, Jay's mother had a stroke, which also sent her into financial distress. She was unable to pay her rent and other bills. Jay, who was twenty-six at the time, decided to pay her rent until she recovered and was able to move to a less expensive area, but his help stopped there. In the past when he'd given her money, she had promised to pay him back but never did. "I know my mom. I know her history with money and jobs. I know what would have happened if I enabled her behavior," he says.

- Shortly after her seventeenth birthday, Julie's father quit his job and opened his own hardware store. He asked her for cash to help support his venture. Because she'd been working part-time jobs to save up for school, she had the money in the bank. But she didn't just hand it over. She wrote up a contract that described when he would pay her back and with how much interest. Then she gave him the money. "My parents had already provided for us and spent money year after year on our sporting activities. I determined if I could help, I would be glad to, as a way of saying 'thank you.' Also, by lending the money, I would guarantee that I wouldn't spend it and I didn't need it for three years," she says. Her plan worked out: her dad paid her back right on time. "Things worked out in the end, and I am happy that I was able to give my dad a gift to help him out when it was needed," she says.

ACCEPTING A PARENTAL HAND UP

Even more common than Tarah's situation is Will LeFavor's. After graduating from Bentley College with a degree in finance and economics, he started working at a financial planning firm outside of Boston. He quickly realized that, between the high cost of housing and his income of around $50,000, he wouldn't be able to save much money if he rented his own apartment. So he moved back home with his parents, who live within an hour and a half's drive of his office. Instead of feeling strained to pay his bills, he saved up $40,000 over the next four years. That let him make a down payment on a three-bedroom home at age twenty-six. At the same time, he continued to put around 10 percent of his income into his 401(k). In addition to the financial boost, he enjoyed the chance to hang out with his parents, retired educators. He says he doesn't worry too much about the stigma that used to surround living with parents as a twenty-something, because it's become more common. Plus, he says, "If I lived on my own, I wouldn't be eating so well!"

Like the Hewsons, Will's parents are happy with the arrangement. "If he was out drinking and partying, I might have second thoughts, but he really does have a plan in place," says Will's sixty-year-old father, Phil. "We said, 'You can stay here as long as you want.'"

That's an offer a lot of us are hearing—and accepting. One in four single twenty-five- to twenty-nine-year-olds lives with his or her parents, and one in five thirty- to thirty-four-year-olds does so.[7]

Along with their homes, parents also share their cash: almost four in ten adults who are sixty or over give money to their adult children.[8] Research shows that, on average, parents give their kids $38,000, in the form of cash, tuition payments, food, housing, and other gifts, between ages eighteen and thirty-four, or about $2,200 a year.[9] "As a historian, I can tell you no older generation in history has ever spent so many resources on grown kids," says Stephanie Coontz, director of research for the Council on Contemporary Families.

What do all these handouts mean? Frank Furstenberg, chair of the academic group Network on Transitions to Adulthood and professor of sociology at the University of Pennsylvania, says that researchers haven't quite gotten to the bottom of the trend toward what he calls "delayed adulthood." But there are some primary suspects. One of them is that people tend to get more education now, which means they are more likely to still be in school in their early twenties and beyond. "That has an effect on when they're ready to settle down," he says. Also, since our life spans are so much longer now than they were a century ago, we don't feel as rushed into establishing a home and family, since we have more time. Housing costs also play a role, which partly explains why young adults in the Northeast have the highest rates of living at home.[10]

Furstenberg says that all this support from parents could ultimately convince young adults to put off having families of their own because they see how expensive it is for their own parents. One possibility, he says, is that "more and more young adults will opt out of becoming parents, partly because it's a daunting task now."

There are plenty of reasons to turn down help from parents, as hard as it is to refuse an outstretched hand full of cash. It's a rare parent who doesn't expect something—even a commitment to future Sunday night dinners—in return for a down payment contribution or a graduate school tuition payment. If it's just about spending time together around the dinner table, that might pose no problem. But sometimes parents want more: they want you to buy a certain kind of house, in a certain kind of neighborhood, or to attend a specific school, and pursue a particular career path. "Parents often look at their kids, expecting to see miniature versions of themselves, and they sometimes use the money as a reward or punishment," says Jon Gallo, coauthor of *The Financially Intelligent Parent*. (If either side suspects any such expectations, he recommends talking about it beforehand, so all parties know what they're getting into.)

☑ Quick Tip: Keeping Credit Separate

Whether you're receiving financial help or giving it, make the transaction without getting mixed up in anyone else's credit record. That means not sharing a credit card, auto loan, or mortgage with anyone else (other than a significant other with whom you'd like to be financially intertwined). Cosigning for a loan instead of handing over cash might seem like a cheap way of helping a friend or relative out, but doing so places you at risk for financial ruin if the other person fails to make future payments.

You might also want to make sure that your parents can afford the help they're offering. Overly generous parents sometimes set themselves up for financial stress—and dependency on their children—later. One Ameriprise Financial survey found that about 30 percent of baby boomers said that the money they had given to their adult children negatively affected their own retirement savings, but most hadn't considered the impact it was having.[11]

☑ Quick Tip: Taxing Gifts

You can give and receive up to $13,000 a year without paying taxes on the gift. After that point, the IRS considers the donor responsible for paying all necessary taxes. (Tuition and medical costs are excluded from that limit.) Also, unless loans carry interest at the prevailing rate set by the Treasury Department, they can be considered gifts for tax purposes—so don't give out any interest-free loans worth more than $13,000 without first thinking of the tax implications.

Phil LeFavor, Will's dad, says that he's already aware that he'll need to limit the financial help he provides at some point, even though he says his wife would happily give endless amounts of support to their two sons. (They do agree that they will be sure to treat each of their sons equally, an approach that is strongly recommended by family experts.) LeFavor, a retired high school vice principal, and his wife live off of a fixed pension that comes from their years of working in the Massachusetts school system. Says Phil, "If he just needs another $30,000 [for a down payment], I can help some, but you have to understand, we could live to be ninety. I can't sell the farm. . . . We have to remain sensible about our financial plan for the future, too."

MY MOM, MY BANK

One way to avoid draining your parents' accounts while still benefiting from their generosity is to pay them back in full, plus interest. Peer-to-peer lending sites such as Virgin Money (virginmoneyus.com) and Prosper (prosper.com) make it easy for friends and family members to officially loan money to each other without needing to calculate taxes on their own or suffer through awkward discussions about the logistics of repayment. After agreeing on an interest rate, you can set up repayment schedules and arrange for automatic payments. Any taxes are calculated just as they would be for a regular bank loan.

That's how Stephen Martin, a thirty-five-year-old technology consultant in Jersey City, bought his first house. When he first started house hunting, he realized he couldn't afford much on his salary. Then his mom, Nancy Flint, a dentist in her early sixties, suggested that they look into peer-to-peer lending, so he could have more money for his house and she could lock in a decent rate of return on her own savings. "Paying interest back to my mom instead of a bank just seemed really appealing to me," he says.

He soon found a one-bedroom place in Jersey City, and, after making a 10 percent down payment, he took out a $405,000 mortgage from his mom through Virgin Money to cover the rest. While he was initially worried that she might try to encourage him to buy a certain type of place since she had a financial stake in the purchase, the only difficult part turned out to be negotiating the interest rate. They settled on 6 percent, which they renegotiated to 5 percent after rates dropped. Stephen was also able to skip the loan origination fees and private mortgage insurance (usually required when down payments are below 20 percent). In total, he estimates that he saved around $15,000. His $2,500 monthly payment is automatically deducted each month and his mom gets a check. "It's been completely trouble free," says Stephen.

His mom agrees. "I'm sixty, so I thought it was good not to have so much in stocks. A portion of my portfolio is now in an investment that brings me a set interest rate and nobody is going to default. It feels safe and it feels good."

Exercises: Family Matters

1. Consider the various ways that you could team up with family members in a mutually beneficial way. Are there skills you could trade? Would sharing a roof make sense? Before acting on these ideas, make sure you all have similar expectations and experiment with a trial period.

2. Talk to your parents about their money situation. Do they expect to be able to support themselves in retirement, or will they likely need some assistance? Are they expecting assistance from you?

3. Evaluate your own level of dependency on your parents. Do you still accept money from them? Does any money exchanged between you affect your relationship? Are you happy with whatever habits you've developed, or do you want to make a change?

4. If anyone—friends, parents, siblings—regularly relies on you for financial support, ask yourself whether you are really helping them or enabling poor financial habits. If the support is straining your own budget, consider whether you need to learn to say no.

7

LESSONS IN MODERN FRUGALITY

As the most recent recession roared into high gear, simplicity came back into style. It became cooler to drive a compact hybrid car than a new SUV. DIY crafting came back into style. Eating in and skipping the trendy new restaurants no longer seemed boring—it seemed smart. The only problem was that members of a generation brought up on takeout and Target weren't entirely sure of themselves in the kitchen or craft store. We had to teach ourselves the skills that our parents, for the most part, never had to learn. In the process, many of us discovered that we not only benefited from the savings but also enjoyed our new talents. And our homes never looked, or smelled, so inviting.

In this chapter, you'll learn the following:

1. Why so many people are choosing simplicity over consumerism

2. The lost lessons of home economics

3. What skills are worth mastering yourself—and what tasks you should outsource

CHOOSING SIMPLICITY

Tim Kasser, a bearded, forty-something professor of psychology at Knox College in western Illinois, works a reduced schedule so he can spend more time writing, working in his garden, playing the piano, and spending time with his wife and two sons. His wife, a psychotherapist, makes a similar choice, working fifteen to twenty hours a week, and only for about half the year. "The extra money I'd get from teaching those other classes isn't worth it to me. It isn't what I want out of life," Tim explains.

In some ways, their lifestyle is more consistent with that of people in the 1930s than the way people live today. They grow much of their own food on their ten acres of land, have goats and chickens that give them milk and eggs, and rarely watch television. (They do have one TV in the basement so their sons can watch a half hour of PBS each day.) For birthdays, they usually give each other coupons for experiences, such as favorite meals or back rubs, rather than purchased gifts. For his sons' birthdays, Tim typically gives them a special day with him, such as a trip to the local water park. Neither Tim nor his wife grew up living this way, but they both discovered they found it far more satisfying than the pursuit of material luxuries.

In his academic work, Tim studies such "voluntary simplicity," which about 10 to 15 percent of Americans pursue. "It means a real awareness and thoughtfulness about how one is living one's life, as opposed to automatically following along," says Tim, author of *The High Price of Materialism*. "One has to think harder about 'How much do I really want to work? Do I want to have a television? What should I be purchasing?'" At the same time, he adds, voluntary simplicity doesn't have to involve much in the way of sacrifice. In fact, it usually means more time for the things you actually want to be doing, such as hanging out with your significant other or hiking in a nearby park.

Tim has found that people who consider themselves to be voluntary simplifiers are happier. In a comparison of two hundred voluntary simplifiers with two hundred mainstream Americans, the simplifiers reported being more satisfied with their lives and having a greater number of pleasant emotions and fewer negative ones. Their incomes, though, were only about two-thirds of the mainstreamers', underscoring the notion that money doesn't always bring happiness.[1]

☑ Quick Tip: Better Gift Giving

The amount of money people say they intend to spend on Christmas gifts has been steadily declining since 2001, pollster John Zogby reports, suggesting that the idea of simplicity is catching on.[2] Consider joining that movement by making your gifts more meaningful and less expensive. Stay away from the pricey jewelry, new cars, and LCD televisions. Instead, opt for cookbooks, museum dates, or the promise of an afternoon spent together. You can also consult websites like craftster.org to find unique DIY gift ideas.

Doreen Orion, a psychiatrist in her late forties, stumbled onto her simplified lifestyle almost by accident. Her husband, Timothy Justice, also a psychiatrist, came home one day a few years ago and said he wanted them to take a break from their jobs and hardworking lifestyle in Boulder and travel around the country in a bus for a year. At first, she strongly resisted, but she eventually agreed to go along. They moved from their dream house into a 340-square-foot bus and visited forty-seven states, including Alaska. Along the way, they survived a nudist RV park, a fire, and even an armed robbery, all of which she ended up writing about in her memoir, *Queen of the Road.*

When they got back home, she says, "We realized that our normal lives were going to start again, and were both hit with this overwhelming sense of dread." Living so minimally had put a spark back in their lives. Doreen decided that her two hundred pairs of shoes, shopaholic tendencies, and dream house weren't making her happy.

She also started to realize the correlation between her shopping and her work: "Every purchase I make, I think, 'That's ten more minutes of work I have to do. I don't think so.'"

So she and Timothy decided to make their new lifestyle permanent, and they recently put their home on the market. They calculated that if they sold their home and lived in their bus, while working occasionally, they could support themselves. "In that 340-square-foot bus, we were happier than we'd ever been in our lives," she says.

Tim Kasser and Doreen Orion are joined by a growing number of Americans who are opting for this brand of downsizing, driven in part by the tougher economic times. In one of her surveys, trend spotter Faith Popcorn found that 90 percent of respondents said they were considering options for a "simpler life," and 84 percent were inclined to buy "less stuff." Part of the impetus, Popcorn says, is that people are tired of the excess consumption that defined much of the 1990s and early 2000s (remember *Clueless*?), and they welcomed the downturn as an opportunity to stop.

Fellow trend spotter Marian Salzman noticed a shift in her own feelings on a recent trip to Europe. While she had previously enjoyed shopping, she suddenly felt as if there was something garish about it, whether it was at a cheaper store like Zara or a local artisan boutique. When she shared her feelings with friends, they said they felt the same way. "There is a total anti-bling thing going on," she says. "We all just have so much complexity in our lives and so much damn stuff, that if consumerism means it's something else I have to put away or figure out how to store and organize, I don't want it." Meanwhile, she adds, "It's become super fashionable to have no-cost weekends where you spend as little as possible, reusing things you have, from board games to the ten-year-old hot tub, cooking at home, drinking cheap wine, and eating stews." Even her wealthy friends seemed suddenly more interested in giving back through charity and becoming closer to their communities. "That whole sense of what's important has really changed," she says.

Pollster John Zogby predicts that the shift will become even more pronounced over the next decade, regardless of economic recovery. By 2020, he says, Americans will be more "Zen like." He explains, "There will be less rushing and traffic, simply because we can't sustain it but also because our lifestyle is changing. . . . People will be working hard and conducting their business, obviously, but working will involve a lot of part-time." It sounds like the balance Tim Kasser and Doreen Orion have already embraced. Even though most people won't be able to shift to a two-thirds schedule or quit their jobs and live in an RV, almost anyone can make small changes, starting in the kitchen.

☑ Quick Tip: Affordable Romance

Alpha Consumer readers suggest the following ideas for cheap date nights:
- Spend the night sketching portraits of each other. (Watch *Titanic* for inspiration from Leonardo DiCaprio and Kate Winslet.)
- Go for a walk.
- Visit lounges that offer free dance lessons. (This one works especially well for single guys looking to pick up ladies, since women tend to outnumber men at these events.)
- Have a picnic in the park.
- Cook dinner and play board games.
- Go to a lecture or performance at your local college.
- Watch a model rocket launch (local clubs can let you know when and where).
- Browse a bookstore.

HOME ECONOMICS 101

The smell of the lentil stew that's simmering on the stove permeates Kate and Thomas Deriso's light-filled condo in Sterling, Virginia, around lunchtime. Before offering me a sample, Kate, thirty-nine, a holistic health counselor, gives me a brief tour of their kitchen: the jar of homegrown alfalfa sprouts, the freezer full of leftovers (she calls it her "fast food" restaurant), the turquoise teapot she uses to make specialty green teas so she can skip Starbucks. She and Thomas, a forty-year-old wholesale food seller, spend no more than $150 a week on their entire food budget, while managing to eat more like Wolfgang Puck than the star of *Super Size Me*. They make their own breakfasts, lunches, and dinners and rarely eat out, because they've discovered they can make better meals themselves. "We would literally sit there [at a restaurant] and say, 'We would be so much better staying at home and taking the time to put our own dinner together. We would have gotten a lot better food for a lot less money,'" says Kate.

On most weekday evenings, Kate preps one of her favorite go-to-meals, such as a chicken and olive one-pot dish or quesadillas with refried beans, while Thomas sits a few feet in front of her, in the living room, watching the news. The open layout of their condo means they can talk and have a glass of wine together while one of them is working in the kitchen. (For the most part, Kate cooks and Thomas cleans, although Thomas specializes in stuffed artichokes and marinara sauce.) "Because of our busy schedules, we don't always see each other, so this is just a great way to communicate and nourish our marriage," says Kate.

For Kate, the kitchen has always been familiar territory. Her mom taught her to cook, make her own peanut butter and salad dressings, and freeze leftovers. "It's been ingrained in me," she says.

Unlike Kate, many of us grew up with parents who preferred to spend as much time out of the kitchen as possible—or with parents who simply did not see cooking as a family activity. That partly explains why the Food Network, food blogs, and books on cooking from scratch have taken off in the last few years—people need to teach themselves these skills because they never learned them as kids. Jed Lyons, chief executive of the Rowman & Littlefield Publishing Group, says he started reissuing decades-old books on topics such as bread making after noticing a spike in demand. "Americans are looking for good, practical information about how to live a more sustainable life, how to save money by doing things like growing their own vegetables . . . and really returning to a way of living that was common for their grandparents," he says.

☑ Quick Tip: Cheap Eats

There's been some debate over whether it really is cheaper to eat at home, or if by the time you buy spices and All-Clad you might as well have gone out for a steak at Morton's. Back in 2002, the *Wall Street Journal* argued that cooking at home actually costs more— but it used $20 bottles of champagne vinegar and $10 mushrooms to make its case. As many letters to the editor pointed out, you don't need Prada-priced ingredients to get a high-class meal.[3] As long as you listen to the suggestions of food bloggers and websites such as allrecipes.com, cookingwithamy.blogspot.com, and bakingandbooks.com, you can learn how to make good, cheap food relatively easily.

The return to the kitchen roughly coincides with the collapse of the Internet bubble and the events of September 11, which made staying home more appealing. Every year since 2001, the number of meals that people have prepared and consumed at home has ticked upward. In 2009, it reached 872 per year, or about 2.4 per day, compared to 835, or 2.3 per day, in 2001. Harry Balzer, vice president of the market research company NPD Group and author of the annual report "Eating Patterns in America," says the increase can't be entirely attributed to economics, although that has a lot to do with it. Gender dynamics also play a role. Men are much more likely to whip up a meatloaf today than they were thirty years ago, when he first started studying these numbers. While women cooked the vast majority of meals in the 1980s, men now cook about 13 percent of dinners prepared at home.

When planning your meals for the week—the best defense against 9 p.m. takeout orders that end up costing $40—look for easy substitutions that don't force you to sacrifice gourmet tastes. Tilapia can replace halibut, and certain casseroles can be just as mouthwatering as steak. Skipping meat altogether, at least a few nights each week, will also reduce your shopping bill. For protein, take advantage of eggs, which can be turned into soufflés and stratas. Beans are another useful ingredient; they can bulk up pasta sauces and soups or be served with rice or quinoa. Plan to reuse leftovers; extra rice can make fried rice the following night. Grate your own cheese and make your own hummus by throwing a can of chickpeas, tahini, garlic, and olive oil into a food processor. It will taste so much better than the store-bought stuff. And don't forget to make extra portions, which can go into the freezer for a quick future meal.

The rediscovery of the domestic arts isn't just about eating. We're also playing with our Wiis in the family room, investing in crafty projects, and even taking on more home improvement work. Martha Stewart, who used to symbolize excess and almost nuttiness when it came to housekeeping, seems to have become the person we all want to emulate. Her *Encyclopedia of Crafts* quickly became a best seller when it was released in early 2009. "People are hungry for knowledge on how they can do things themselves," says Robbie Blinkoff, principal anthropologist at Context-Based Research Group, which follows consumer trends.

So, how to get started? If you have a Friday night martini habit, as my husband and I do, consider buying a jar of olives and some vodka and teaching yourself how to shake one up. (My husband's martinis can now beat any restaurants' offerings.) Or try making coffee according to the advice of Ina Garten, of *Barefoot Contessa* fame: use only one rounded tablespoon of coffee for every two cups of water. If you're not going to drink the coffee immediately, pour it into an insulated thermos. Leaving the coffee in the pot on the heated pad will turn it bitter within a half hour or so. If you follow her steps, your homemade brew will be better than most of the stuff you can buy in cafes. Cutting hair at home, biking to work, and staying in for movie night are other popular options.

☑ Quick Tip: Frugal Flashback

Sometimes, we have to look back a generation or two for frugality lessons. My grandparents, who raised their four sons, including my dad, during the World War II rations era in England, wore clothes until they became threadbare. They darned their socks. They grew vegetables in their backyard. When they took baths, they used no more than four or five inches of water. They reused plastic bags, rinsing them out and drying them in the sink. Every bit of a leftover roast chicken would go into future meals, including the bones, for flavoring soups.

In his book *Railwayman's Son*, Hugh Hawkins, my former history professor at Amherst College, describes how his mother brainstormed ways she could bring in extra income, such as opening a restaurant or raising chickens. In her Great Depression memoir *Little Heathens: Hard Times and High Spirits on an Iowa Farm During the Great Depression*, author Mildred Armstrong Kalish recalls making leather, quilts, bread, and soap from scratch. And in *My Own Two Feet*, children's author Beverly Cleary describes a delectable dish known as "smells to heaven" casserole, a simple meal that brought everyone together for dinner.

If this is starting to sound a bit too *Little House on the Prairie* for you, consider that the most glamorous celebrities are leading the way. Gwyneth Paltrow shared one of her favorite Sunday night dinner recipes, featuring spaghetti and meatballs, with readers of her newsletter, GOOP. Victoria Beckham (aka "Posh Spice") and Heidi Klum don't hide the fact that they shop at Target, which has been promoting the do-it-yourself trend, for their kids.

For extra motivation, start a friendly competition with your significant other. That's how yoga studio owner Annie Mahon got over her penchant for impulse shopping. She and her husband challenged each other to see who could hold off buying anything new the longest. (Groceries, medicine, and necessary purchases for their four children were excluded.) Soon, Annie, who's in her mid-forties, started putting the catalogs that came with each day's mail directly into the recycling bin instead of spending time wondering if she should buy anything from them. "It feels great, because afterwards, there's no residual feeling of, 'Oh, I wish I had gotten this.' So far, it doesn't feel like I'm missing anything. It feels like I'm gaining," she says. Six weeks into the competition, she estimated that she had already saved at least $1,000. She enjoyed the change so much that she and her husband decided to permanently spend less.

The point is simply to spend money on what you most enjoy instead of just watching it disappear. Ben, a thirty-something lawyer in Washington, DC, who works for a nonprofit and earns around $52,000 a year, drives a 1993 Honda Accord with 200,000 miles on it and shares a $1,050 per month studio apartment with his girlfriend, which he furnished with used furniture through craigslist.org. Each week, he buys a six-pack of bagels and a box of tea and skips the coffee shop, which he estimates saves him around $95 each month. Before meeting up for a night out with friends, he eats a peanut butter and banana sandwich so he doesn't need to buy entrees. Instead, he goes for cheaper appetizers. Those routines let him spend money on traveling: he recently visited Panama and Mexico.

WHEN TO OUTSOURCE

Just because making your own clothes and growing your own pota-
toes is cheaper doesn't mean it's always a good idea. Sometimes paying
extra, especially when it saves you time, is well worth the price. Stephanie Britton, a thirty-four-year-old engineer living outside Atlanta,
hired a once-a-month deep cleaning service after she got married and
moved into a bigger house. She used to spend about four hours at least
once a month vacuuming, dusting, mopping, and waxing the hardwood floors of the five-bedroom home. "At first I felt bad. Since there
are only two people, it shouldn't be too hard to clean up after ourselves.
But my husband doesn't like to clean, at least not to my standards, so
the compromise was to get someone," she says. Now, she doesn't need
to nag her husband, and she spends her extra four hours a month on
activities she enjoys far more than getting the last dust mite out of the
curtains. She volunteers at her church and the local ski club and gets
other errands done. Plus, she says, "It keeps marital happiness."

Erica Douglass, a twenty-nine-year-old entrepreneur based in
San Diego, takes outsourcing one step farther: she hires a personal
assistant who works eight hours a week for about $16 an hour. As a
result, for a little over $500 a month, she never has to worry about her
laundry, keeping up with thank-you notes, doing the dishes, or getting
rid of her clutter on craigslist. "For me, it comes down to 'What is the
most valuable use of time?' My goal is to help millions of people in the
world, and by having a personal assistant, I can more effectively use
my time to help both myself and other people," says Erica, who sold
her online business for over $1 million when she was twenty-six and
now runs a site, erica.biz, where she offers guidance to other entrepreneurs. In fact, if she ever had to cut her budget, Erica says she'd
rather move into a (small) apartment and keep her personal assistant
than give up the help. "It's much more valuable to me to spend money
on people and gain time than to spend money on stuff," she says.

Hiring help often comes with a tax bill—a sticky issue that has tripped up more than one White House cabinet nominee. Federal law requires anyone who employs a household worker to fill out a form to verify his employment eligibility. It's called an I-9, and it can be found at uscis.gov. You don't need to give it to anyone; you just need to have it in your files. If you pay a household worker more than $1,700 a year (the amount goes up annually), then you typically have to pay Social Security and Medicare taxes. Unemployment taxes may also apply. To calculate how much you owe, get a Schedule H form when you file your taxes, and also file W-2 and W-3 forms with the Social Security Administration. In addition, your state may have other requirements for unemployment insurance taxes or workers' compensation.

The assistance has provided such a boost to her productivity that Erica recently decided to start outsourcing even more tasks. She is hiring someone to manage her Twitter followers and decide which ones to follow back, a job that usually takes her about thirty minutes a day. Using odesk.com, which connects freelancers to people looking for help, she found a woman in the Philippines willing to do the tasks for $3.33 an hour. (She's also used elance.com, which provides a similar service.)

Erica recommends smoothing the transition to using hired help by giving clear instructions. You probably won't save time for the first week or two, she says, as you teach the assistant what you want him or her to do, but the time savings will begin to accrue soon afterward. Erica's hot tub, for example, requires weekly maintenance, which is one of her assistant's jobs. Erica spent an hour creating a binder explaining exactly how to go about cleaning it, which means she can now forget about the task completely and trust her assistant to do exactly what she wants, saving her about twenty minutes each week. As for making sure she hires people who do high-quality work, she usually asks them to complete a test project before she commits to hiring them. If someone turns out to be a bad fit, she recommends firing them and moving on—this is an employee, not a best friend.

> ### ☑ Quick Tip: Delegating Your Chore List
>
> Make a list of the tasks you spend time on each week. It might include laundry, cleaning the house, driving kids around, responding to emails, answering the phone, organizing the closet, and cooking. Keep track of how much time you spend on each one over the course of a month. Then, make a second list of what else you could be doing with that time. Working on your book? Designing your dream house? Playing Scrabble with your husband? Do a little online research to see how much it would cost to hire someone to do the chores for you, and then do a little cost-benefit analysis. A cleaning service, for example, might cost $80 per visit, and save you four hours. If you would pay $20 an hour to do whatever is on your second list, then the investment is worth it. Consider hiring help, at least on a trial basis. Of course, keep your yearly budget in mind when making this decision—if you aren't saving enough for retirement and other goals now, then maybe that $20 game of Scrabble can wait.

Given the time-consuming nature of housework—the University of Michigan's Institute for Social Research estimates that married women spend around seventeen hours a week on it, and married men spend about seven—it's no surprise that people like Stephanie and Erica decide to outsource it.[4] Many higher-income people do. According to the Consumer Expenditure Survey, households earning over $70,000 a year spend an average of $890 on household services, compared to $400 for households earning between $50,000 and $70,000.[5]

Craig Lair, an assistant professor of sociology at Gettysburg College who has studied domestic outsourcing, says a household hiring help is no different from companies outsourcing their payroll operations so they can focus on their main businesses. "People are using outsourcing so they can concentrate on their core activities, however they define them," he explains. For some people, that's work and family; for others, it's gardening. He's noticed an increase in the popularity of hiring lawn care services, for example, while people are also spending more money on do-it-yourself gardening projects. People want to outsource the grunt work, he says, so they can focus on the fun part of growing stuff. For me, that means paying for a grocery delivery service, since I can't stand food shopping, but doing all of my own cooking, since I find sautéing onions as relaxing as getting a hot stone massage.

Exercises: Return to Frugality

1. Consider ways you could simplify your life in order to free up extra money and time, which you could put toward something you enjoy more. Do you want to watch less television and cancel cable, or bike to work instead of driving? Blogs on the pursuit of simplicity, such as smallnotebook.org, can provide inspiration.

2. Examine your gift-giving habits. Were the last few things you gave to friends or family members meaningful? How would an afternoon spent wandering through a museum with that person, followed by coffee, have compared?

3. Try planning your meals for a week. Can you coordinate the meals so you end up reusing leftovers, such as turning a roast chicken into pizza toppings the following night? Or make some of the prepared food that you would normally purchase, such as hummus or grated cheese? For simple ideas, check out food blogs and websites. *How to Cook Everything*, by Mark Bittman, is another good resource, especially for beginners.

4. Take a look at your household chores. What would you rather pay someone to do for you? How would you spend that extra time, and is it worth the cost of the service? Don't forget to include tips and taxes in your calculations.

8

LOVE, RINGS, AND MORTGAGES

It's a well-known scenario: Girl and guy fall in love. They move in together. Maybe they decide to buy a house. Then, tedious discussions of how to share utility bills and mortgage payments slowly replace romantic dates. They break up. Anger and confusion ensue as they try to untangle their finances.

Living together, marriage, and home ownership raise a slew of sticky relationship issues: Should the higher earner shoulder more of the rent? Do individual savings accounts become joint property? Is buying a home together a good idea?

In this chapter, you will learn the following:

1. How to manage money with a significant other

2. How to prepare financially for marriage

3. Why the traditional advice on how and when to house-hunt is wrong

I LOVE YOU, YOU'RE PERFECT,
NOW LET'S MOVE IN TOGETHER

When Pasha Carroll, twenty-nine, and her boyfriend, Matthew Krise, thirty, first moved into a one-bedroom Chicago apartment together after a year of dating, they came up with a financial system that kept most of their money separate. Pasha, a writer and bartender, and Matt, a student and waiter, maintain separate bank accounts and pay their own bills, including student loan and credit card debt. They split joint expenses: rent, groceries, and other living costs are divided evenly. Matt covers dinners out, and Pasha cooks. When they go on vacation, Matt buys the plane tickets and Pasha pays for the accommodations. "We never have to squabble or ask each other for money," Pasha says. The fact that they're both relatively frugal also helps.

As unromantic as it sounds, couples often decide that keeping their money separate, at least until they get married or have a lifelong commitment, is better both for the relationship and for their finances. If accounts are combined, the risk of something going wrong in the event of a breakup is high: one person could withdraw all the money out of a joint savings account and the other would have no protection. If both names are on a car lease and one person stops paying, even if that person is the primary owner of the car, the other person's credit score can be ruined as well. (The credit bureaus won't care that you broke up three months ago and haven't spoken since.) Any joint investments in shared assets—such as a kitchen renovation for a condo—can be lost if only one person's name is on the title. Legalities aside, a lot of couples say they like the independence of having two accounts anyway, at least before they decide they've found their permanent soul mate.

Newlyweds who earn similar, high salaries often get an unwelcome surprise the year after they get married: they find themselves stuck with a mega-tax bill. That's because the so-called marriage penalty still exists in the upper tax brackets. In 2010, for example, husbands and wives who each earn $68,650 and up in taxable income are at risk for paying more married than they did as singletons. Earnings above that amount face a 28 percent tax, compared to 25 percent pre-marriage. Couples are most at risk when they bring home similar incomes. (The reverse is also true. When one person in the marriage brings home all or most of the money in a marriage, that couple usually gets a tax break.) The best way to prepare for this unwelcome wedding "gift" is to know it's coming and to deduct more from your salary throughout the year to avoid a large bill on April 15.

Even with that degree of separation, additional protective measures sometimes make sense. Talking about how you would split things up if you decided to go your separate ways can prevent bad surprises later. Unless children or major assets are involved, there's usually no need to hire a lawyer. In fact, you can just write down the answers to these questions along with any others that apply: Who would stay in the apartment? Who would get the cats? The car? If you want to formalize the process, you can pay a nominal fee to download forms, such as a living-together guide and contract, at nolo.com. Since unmarried couples don't get to argue their case in divorce court, it could be your only protection in place if things go south. (The legal ramifications of common-law marriages, civil unions, and domestic partnerships vary by state.)

Couples might also want to consider talking about any debts, past bankruptcy filings, and credit report problems, because even if you're not legally liable for your girlfriend's $50,000 student loan, it could end up affecting your quality of life if 10 percent of the household income goes toward paying it off each month.

It's okay to say no when you receive wedding invitations—especially if the nuptials will be taking place in exotic locations such as the Caribbean. Condé Nast's brides.com estimates that 16 percent of nuptials are now destination weddings, which means guests usually have to pay for expensive airplane flights as well as resort costs, along with using up some of their precious vacation days. Bridesmaids and groomsmen are hit with a double whammy: they are also often responsible for buying or renting outfits, purchasing matching shoes, and, for bridesmaids, paying for professional hair and nail services (not to mention hosting prewedding celebrations such as showers and bachelor or bachelorette parties.) In fact, theknot.com estimates that, on average, bridesmaids pay close to $700 for the honor. If you'd rather spend the money elsewhere, then consider declining the invitation, because even the most demanding couples deserve the support of people who truly want to be there.

When you add real estate to the equation, the level of preparation required for purchasing a home rivals that of planning for a presidential inauguration. Even if one person puts more money into the down payment and mortgage payments, couples may want to consider having both names on the title. Otherwise, the other person's hard work refinishing the basement or landscaping the backyard could net him or her no return. At the same time, if one person is making a larger financial commitment, he or she deserves to protect his investment, too. One way to do that is to spell out that the larger contributor gets to keep more in the event of a breakup or can reimburse the lesser earner for that person's contributions.

"I see it happening too often—a couple gets together, says 'I love you, let's set up house and make this official'. . . and then [one person] signs away half of their equity," says Sheryl Garrett, a certified financial planner based in Shawnee Mission, Kansas, and author of *Money Without Matrimony*. Couples also need to talk about who would get the first opportunity to purchase the house if they were to break up, at what price would they sell it, and how many days they would have to refinance the mortgage in their own name. That kind of advance planning can protect the more passive member of the couple, or somebody who feels guilty for abandoning a relationship and might otherwise end up walking away from what's rightfully his or hers. (Sans any sort of written agreement, the laws on who gets what vary by state.)

Just talking about these "what-ifs" can provide insight into the future of a relationship. In fact, that's exactly what happened to Sheryl. As she and her former significant other debated those financial details, they ended up deciding that they didn't want to live together after all. "It forces a conversation about stuff that most couples don't have until long after you get married," she says.

Sometimes, that conversation affirms the strength of a relationship. When Janet Parkinson, a freelance writer and editor in her early forties, bought a condo with her boyfriend, a facilities manager, in Boston ten years ago, they invested similar amounts of money and decided to take turns paying the mortgage to keep things equal. They also put both their names on the title and gave each other the right of survivorship, so if one person died the other would still own the house—something that happens automatically for married couples. After about four years of living in a condo together, they decided to move into a bigger house. The day they made the offer, her boyfriend proposed, and they've been living happily in their house ever since. "Being with someone who shares your financial values will let you avoid a lot of issues," Janet says.

Pasha and Matt's story also has a happy ending. After three years of living together, they got engaged. Now, as they plan their wedding, they're splitting the cost of the celebration, and they plan to keep separate accounts even after they walk down the aisle. Pasha explains, "We just have not had the need to combine our finances." Next on their agenda: buying a home together.

Here are five things to do before moving in with your significant other:

1. Talk about how you want to share household expenses. Will the person who earns a higher salary contribute more toward the cost of groceries and rent?
2. Discuss how much credit card debt you each have.
3. If you plan to share a house or car, put the specifics of the arrangement in writing. Who will keep it if you break up? If only one person's name is on the title, is the other person expected to pay for repairs and upkeep?
4. Decide if you want to create a shared bank account to pay for joint expenses or operate along a strictly his-hers line of separation.
5. Share your financial goals and discuss where you each plan to be in five years. Do you want to prioritize paying off debt or traveling to Tahiti? Is saving up for a down payment more of a priority than eating at high-end restaurants?

MARRIED, WITH BENEFITS

Getting married can have as large an impact on your finances as your career choice. The simple act of tying the knot can change your tax status, your assets, your debt loads, and your income overnight. You could discover that you and your spouse have vastly different spending habits, which weren't apparent during those early date nights. You might find out about a latent credit card balance that's been building up. And you could suddenly find yourself the sole household earner if your partner goes back to school, loses a job, or takes time off to have a baby. You might even become unexpectedly responsible for your partner's extended family's financial stresses. Talking over these topics ahead of time in a neutral place, like a coffee shop or therapist's office, can make for a much smoother first year of marriage.

The average wedding now costs close to $25,000. But it doesn't have to. Small changes, such as holding the wedding on a Friday or Sunday instead of a Saturday, chopping the guest list, and relying on the flower arranging and photography talents of friends, can all reduce the cost. After her fiancé temporarily lost his job, Chrissy King, a thirty-one-year-old billing coordinator in Worcester, Massachusetts, turned what was going to be a sit-down dinner into a cocktail reception at an inexpensive church hall. She also cut about twenty-five people from the guest list, bringing the final tally to 140, and hired a coworker to serve as the deejay for $300. Another coworker volunteered as the photographer. She estimates she saved about $6,000.

Here are some questions to get that discussion started:

- Do you prefer to share bank accounts or keep them separate?

- Do you know how each other's spending habits differ?

- Do you know how much debt your partner currently carries, including credit card and student loan debt? Do you have a general sense of the strength of each other's credit report?

- Could you describe each other's career dreams and financial plans? Do you know if the other person wants to go back to school, make a major career change, or be a stay-at-home parent one day?

- Do you know how you would each respond to a request from a family member or friend for money?

- Do you feel comfortable with the other person inheriting your assets in the event of your death?

- Do you know how the assets you bring into the marriage will be divided in the event of divorce?

Even if you have all those questions sorted out, marriage can trigger a series of unexpected financial consequences. It can push two big earners into a higher tax bracket than either one would face as a singleton. It can also lower tax bills, since married couples can share deductions for mortgage payments, children, and other expenses. Being married also generally allows couples to share health insurance plans, which usually creates significant savings.

There's also evidence that something about marriage itself creates wealth. Studies have found that people are more likely to save money when they're married and couples who have been married for a long time tend to build up more wealth compared to those who have not.[1]

☑ Quick Tip: Smart Registries

The very nature of wedding registries can sometimes seem a bit crass. You are essentially asking people to give you money, or the Crate & Barrel equivalent. But there is a way to get what you want—and the stuff that will help you the most financially—without seeming overly greedy. First, do register. Sometimes, people think, "I just want people to give me money, so I won't register and people will take the hint." No, they won't. You will end up with a dozen crystal bowls that are not returnable. Second, when you register, consider items that are useful and will last—but not the way china plates last, which is in a box in your closet. Think about skipping the traditional silver and china settings and going instead for the items you would have to buy for yourself anyway: sheets, luggage, everyday kitchen items. As tempting as it is, try to avoid registering for money in the form of gift certificates to travel destinations. It can rub traditionalists the wrong way. And don't worry—a certain percentage of your guests will end up giving you money anyway, which you can graciously accept.

As for how that money is best handled, couples take vastly different approaches. A few months before Kellie and Dan Mercurio, now both in their early thirties, got married, they started talking about whether they should keep separate or joint accounts. On one hand, they viewed marriage as a partnership. There was no question that they would need a joint checking account for household bills and expenses. "We knew my money was his money and his money was my money the day we said, 'I do,'" explains Kellie, who worked as a bank manager before becoming a stay-at-home mom. But on the other hand, they were both used to managing their own money. "For someone who is somewhat of a control freak, it's hard to say, 'Okay, let's have everything coming out of one account,'" says Dan, who works in financial sales in the Boston area.

So they settled on a hybrid solution that involves four accounts. One joint account is dubbed the "operating account." The bulk of their household income goes in there and pays for joint expenses, including the mortgage, utility bills, and dinners out. Then, Kellie and Dan each have a separate personal account. She pays for her nails; he pays for his hair cuts. Lastly, they have a joint savings account.

Aside from the independence that having separate accounts gives them, Dan and Kellie say it also helps them stay organized and keep track of how money is being spent. "We're probably polar opposites in the way that we track and register money. I'm paper-based, and he just has a general understanding of how much is in the account. It drives me crazy. It was easier for us to do it this way than to keep track of little daily items," says Kellie.

Q. My husband spends more money in a day than I do in a week. His splurges—and credit card debt—drive me crazy. How can I protect my own financial security?
A. As long as he continues to overspend, it will be difficult. Even if your name isn't on his credit cards (and it shouldn't be, because in the event that you end up divorcing, you don't want to be responsible for his debt), his habits still affect your life. They determine how much house you can buy, what interest rate you can get on a car loan, and what kind of vacation you can afford. The only way to keep his spending tendencies from ruining your own financial life is to change them. If you can't do it alone, visit a therapist—the hourly fee will pay for itself quickly.

Dan agrees. "Kellie likes receipts for everything. That's a hard habit for me. Now, if I don't have a receipt from my haircut, I don't have to argue about that." If Kellie wants to check in, she just logs onto their online account and tracks spending that way. Plus, Dan adds, "If she wants to splurge on something, she can do it without asking me." They also don't make any distinctions on spending power based on who earns more. "Just because I get a larger direct deposit does not mean that I have an increased spending limit," explains Dan. "Our money is our money."

About half of households now have multiple checking accounts, up from 40 percent in 2001, which suggests that separate accounts for husbands and wives are becoming increasingly popular.[2] As women earn more money (around one in three now earns more than her husband[3]) and couples marry later, the desire to maintain financial independence after marriage seems to have grown.

Sharon Epperson, a correspondent for CNBC in her early forties, and her husband keep separate spending accounts so she doesn't worry about the regular stream of items that her husband orders from Amazon or the spa treatments that she schedules for herself. Sharon, who writes about marriage and finances in her book *The Big Payoff*, says separate accounts make sense for many couples, especially where each person is used to having control. "I think it can help relieve some of the tension over money," she says. She's quick to add that if one spouse leaves the workforce to care for kids full-time, that person stills need to have as much "fun money" to spend as the spouse in the workforce does.

In fact, some couples say that separate accounts become even more important when one person's income is much greater than the other's, because the lower earner doesn't want to feel beholden to the breadwinner for every expense. Having two accounts, each with an equal amount of spending money, helps avoid that. New York–based relationship therapist Bonnie Eaker Weil explains that no one should ever feel like he or she has to ask permission before buying something. "I call it 'Mother, may I?' You don't want to get into that position where you're the little girl, or you're the little boy, and the other person is your parent. You want to have your own money, and certain things are guilt-free, and you just do what you want with it. If you want to buy a latte, or lipstick, or a facial, you do not have to ask permission, because it's your own money," says Weil.

☑ Quick Tip: The $2,000 Kiss

According to research by therapist Bonnie Eaker Weil, author of *Financial Infidelity*, people often make purchases after fighting with their partners. She dubs these "POP" ("pissed-off purchases") shots. She says the average POP shot is almost $500 and people tend to make them three to four times a year. That means that some people are blowing $2,000 a year because of relationship tension. Her solution is simple: kiss. Because kissing provides a similar dopamine high to the one shopping provides, she says it can replace those splurges at the mall.

For others, the traditional, share-everything approach works best. When Marianne Kayan, a thirty-two-year-old lawyer in Washington, DC, married her husband, they were both in graduate school and had little money. They decided to combine what they had for convenience as well as for what it signified. "Being married is a process of sharing. If there is the trust, and the commitment to sharing a life together, then financial aspects are also part of that sharing," she says. As for their individual splurges, they trust each other to be responsible. "If I spent money on something that was a little bit more than normal, he's usually very supportive," she says.

Clinical psychologist Jack Singer says that kind of attitude can signify a healthy relationship. "When people insist on keeping their own account, that speaks volumes about their feelings. There's something they're not comfortable with or they don't trust" if they're not willing to talk about it, he explains. But if the couple is open with each other, communicates their reasons, and agrees on the advantages for some separateness, then that can strengthen the relationship, he says. And if couples come into a marriage with kids or other major financial obligations, keeping separate accounts to pay for those responsibilities can prevent resentment from building.

Even people who love their separate accounts usually agree that separate doesn't mean secretive. Kellie and Dan, for example, know about the other person's purchases, even if they come from their own checking accounts.

Q. If I get divorced, is my spouse entitled to half of the money that I brought into the marriage, including the inheritance my grandmother left me?

A. The laws vary by state. Some states lean toward considering all property owned during marriage as communal, while others take a more individual approach. Often it depends on whether spouses treat the money as joint or separate—in other words, if they "commingle" it. If a husband and wife are strict about keeping investment accounts that they brought into the marriage separate, then divorce courts will often view them as their individual property. But if both people make deposits to an account, even if it's in only one person's name, it could easily be seen as joint. The same goes for inheritances, although they are more likely to be looked at as individual property, unless the couple commingled the money with other accounts. If this is a topic that concerns you because you're bringing substantial assets into a marriage, perhaps in the form of a home, inheritance, or trust fund, you should talk to a lawyer about how best to protect that money.

HOUSE HUNTING, POST-MORTGAGE CRISIS

The urge to buy a home often coincides with a change in relationship status, and partnerships also affect how much you can afford. When Jane Hodges, a forty-year-old freelance writer in Seattle, was ready to buy her first house, she was single, and she learned that she'd have a better chance of getting approved for a mortgage if she held a full-time job. So she decided to hold on to a contract position at the *Seattle Times* longer than she had expected. "I knew if I stayed, I could qualify for a mortgage," she says. While earning a salary in the mid-$50,000s, she bought a light gray, four-bedroom house for $230,000. Through a Federal Housing Administration program, she put 3 percent down and took out a thirty-year, fixed-rate loan with a 5.1 percent interest rate. "As soon as I bought it, I quit my job. Lenders don't care what you do once you own it," she says. Two years later, when she tried to take out a home equity line of credit to put toward home improvements, she found out just how hard it can be for self-employed people to get loans. Even though her credit score was high and she was earning over $85,000—and her home was appraised at over $320,000—she had a hard time finding a bank to approve her for a $20,000 loan. Eventually, she found one that agreed to give her a loan for up to $60,000, based on her tax records, bank account, and credit.

☑ Quick Tip: Renters Insurance—Worth the Price

Unlike home owners, renters aren't usually required to take out insurance to protect them in the event of fire, flooding, or burglary. But consider taking out a policy anyway. It can run as little as $100 a year, depending on where you live and how much you want to insure. Most insurers let you add clauses (for a fee) for any additional assets you have, such as jewelry. A recent survey by Allstate Insurance found that two in three college-age adults had no renters insurance at all, even though about half valued their belongings at over $10,000. Part of their hesitancy seemed to come from confusion over the cost of renters insurance; one in three thought it cost fifteen times more than it actually does. You can compare prices and get quotes by visiting insurers' websites. Combining it with your auto insurance can make it even cheaper.[4]

Later, when Jane and her now-husband were hunting for a home to buy together, she found herself back in lenders' good graces. Even though she was still working as a freelancer, the fact that her fiancé held a full-time job and had already sold his prior home, which meant he had plenty of savings in the bank, made up for the fact that she was self-employed. "If you're self-employed but paired up with someone else who isn't, it's probably a perk," she says. The couple soon settled into a three-bedroom brick home with hardwood floors and a granite fireplace.

Married or not, anyone thinking about buying a home should check up on his or her credit report to see if any errors need to be fixed, pay down high-interest debt to free up cash for the mortgage payment (car loans are a prime target), and research all the fees involved in taking out a mortgage. A $600,000 home could easily come with over $20,000 in closing costs. You can also educate yourself on which fees can be negotiated and which ones you can shop around for. (The appraisal fee, administrative fee, and title insurance typically come with wiggle room. Hazard insurance and taxes usually do not.)

When my husband and I started shopping for our first house and got an estimate of our mortgage costs from the bank, I was introduced to fees that I had never heard of. There was the $505 application fee. (That was on top of the $395 processing fee.) There was the $175 for an "improvement certification," and the jaw-dropping $10,000 "recordation tax." We also received two different estimates, one that included points and one that didn't. Points, which sound like they refer to some sort of reward system, are actually just one more thing the borrower can pay for. As I found out later, one point essentially equals 1 percent of the loan amount, and borrowers can purchase "points" to decrease the overall interest they end up paying. The more you pay up front, the lower your total loan payments will be.

But before getting knee-deep in those details, you might want to consider whether or not you really want to buy a house. Sure, there's something nice about the idea of going home every night to a three-bedroom ranch home with window treatments you picked out yourself. But consider this: home owners tend to be heavier and more miserable than renters. Researchers at the Wharton School of Business found, after they controlled for household income, housing quality, and health, that home owners aren't any happier than renters, and, in fact, "they report to derive more pain from their house and home." And perhaps because they are so busy updating those window treatments or mowing the lawn, home owners spend less time on leisure activities and with friends, the study found.[5]

☑ Quick Tip: Single, Happy, and Home

For Deborah Pont, a communications professional in her early forties who lives in Stonington, Connecticut, the urge to buy a home of her own came before the one to walk down the aisle. At first, that order of events bothered her. "I got the keys and went to my new house, and it dawned on me: I did something that I thought by my age I'd be doing with my spouse." She called her grandmother and told her how she felt. "She said, 'You know what, you're in a great spot. You should be glad that you can buy a house by yourself. You just shake that right off. Soon you'll be busying yourself with renovations and you'll be glad you don't have to talk to someone else about 'what color should we paint this room' or 'can we afford to replace the cabinets.'" Deb realized that her grandmother was right. "I don't have to ask permission to do anything and don't have to consult with anyone else." When she wants extra opinions, she turns to her friends. In the meantime, she's been busy painting her bedroom and working in her garden.

If that's not enough to turn you off to home ownership, consider this: since the fall of 2007, housing appreciation has been largely negative, according to the Federal Housing Finance Agency.[6] That means that anyone who bought a house before that time has probably lost money on it. (Of course, location has a lot to do with it. The more established neighborhoods of cities have held their value far better than up-and-coming spots have.) In some cases, even a money market fund has paid higher returns than a condo, especially after you consider all the fees and other transaction costs involved.

It's possible that we'll never see housing prices go up like they did during our parents' lifetimes again. While plenty of baby boomers used their homes like ATM machines, taking out home equity loans and downgrading when they needed cash for retirement, there's a good chance that our generation will have to find an alternate funding source. In the meantime, we can avoid falling victim to another housing bubble by not buying homes we can't afford. And the way to make that calculation has changed a lot since the financial crisis.

☑ Quick Tip: The Price of Home Insurance

Title insurance might sound about as useful as wearing a life jacket for a few laps around the swimming pool. Basically, it protects home buyers (and lenders) from the small chance that someone else, such as previous owners or their heirs or a contractor who did work on the home years ago, will make some sort of claim on the property. No one wants to inherit a decades-old plumbing bill.

Lenders usually require you to buy title insurance for their part of the loan, but buyers have more flexibility when it comes to their portion of the home equity. The cost depends on the value of the property, but it can easily run over $1,000 at the time of settlement. Declining it comes with risks, because if someone does have a claim to the property, it's potentially a very expensive problem. According to the American Land Title Association, which represents insurers, one in three properties has some sort of title problem that needs to be fixed before it's sold. (The exact rules regarding title insurance vary by state; in some states, sellers pay for it.)

But just because you opt for the life jacket doesn't mean you have to pay top dollar for it. You can shop around for title insurance from different insurance companies to make sure you're getting the best deal possible, which could save you a few hundred dollars. Of course, when you're paying hundreds of thousands of dollars for a home, that might not sound like much, which is why many people skip comparison shopping altogether. But the difference could at least pay for a lamp for your new home.

First of all, renting is no longer necessarily the same as "throwing money away," as home owners were so fond of saying even just five years ago. If a house loses value, or the buyer loses his job and can no longer afford the monthly payments, then a house quickly turns into an income incinerator. "But what about the tax deduction? At least you can subtract the interest payments from your tax bill," an eager realtor might say. But saving even $500 a month through tax deductions doesn't mean much if you are one day faced with selling your starter home at a loss of $50,000.

Another traditional rule of thumb, that buyers should spend around one-third of their pre-tax income on home ownership, also no longer applies.[7] First of all, it doesn't leave any room for the unexpected, from maternity leaves to job losses to a roof that needs replacing. Second, there's no single percentage that makes sense for everyone, since each household has different priorities and savings goals. If you're already spending one-third of your income on student loans, or day care, then you can probably hardly afford to spend even 20 percent of your pay on your home. Another factor to consider is how long you plan to stay in the home, because selling after less than four or five years means you're also paying for significant transaction expenses (such as closing and moving costs).

A more realistic goal for a home-ownership budget depends on a person's overall spending plan. For some people, one-quarter of their income might make sense; others might feel perfectly comfortable with the traditional 33 percent—or more.

Owning a house also comes with a lot of extra costs that add to the overall bill: repairs and upkeep; transportation, if the house is farther from your job than your rental was; and utilities. And then there's the time factor: home owners spend their Saturdays raking leaves and doing other household chores, they tend to have more rooms to clean than renters do, and they have to stay home from work to wait for the plumber instead of just leaving a note for the landlord about the drippy faucet. That could help explain why home owners aren't always happy, even if they come home to a beautiful house every night. They know what it costs to keep it that way.

Remember our representative couple, Kenneth and Danielle? Three years after saying "I do," they bought a two-bedroom condo in downtown Austin. Now, with Kenneth still working as a business consultant and Danielle employed as an architect, they bring home a combined paycheck of $150,000. Through careful planning, they are able to save around $40,000 a year. They took out $60,000 from their savings for the down payment on the condo, but they've been building that fund back up again and now have close to $50,000 in the bank. Although they initially disagreed about what percentage of their income to save, since Danielle is more likely to want to splurge on a last-minute trip to visit friends in San Francisco or a fancy dinner, they've developed a spend-and-save system that works for them. They pick a handful of luxuries that they both enjoy—bottles of wine, an annual vacation, a big-screen television—and then opt for frugality when it comes to the rest of their lifestyle. That means cooking at home most nights, something they enjoy anyway, and limiting their clothing budgets. They plan to use the money they're saving to upgrade to a larger home as soon as they start a family—a step that will pose a new set of financial challenges.

Exercises: For Richer or Poorer

1. If you are thinking of moving in with your partner, or even if you're already living together, schedule a time to talk about money. Are you each happy with your current arrangement? Do you want to share more, or less? Do you each feel that your household contributions are fair? If necessary, write down how you would divide your assets if you were to break up.

2. If you plan to marry or form a domestic partnership, or have recently done so, consider how you feel about your financial arrangements. Have you talked about what you will keep separate and what you will

combine? Do you have any concerns about what would happen in the event of death or divorce?

3. Take a look at the role money plays in your relationship. Does it give you a sense of shared goals and ambitions, or does it cause tensions or fights? If it's the latter, could you change the way you share money to avoid those fights, such as keeping more of it separate, or agreeing on the same long-term savings goals?

4. Examine your feelings about home ownership. If you're still renting, is buying a house a short-term goal? Or are there enough downsides, in the form of risks and responsibilities, to keep you renting?

9

BABIES AND BANK ACCOUNTS

The typical married couple earning over $98,470 a year spends around $40,000 on their child in the first two years of his life.[1] But that doesn't mean we all have to wait until we have an extra forty grand lying around to start a family. Instead, young professionals are increasingly resisting the typical spending splurges that grip many first time par ents, temporarily reducing retirement savings, and building up baby funds in advance, even before becoming familiar with the term TTC ("trying to conceive").

In this chapter, you'll learn the following:

1. Ways to flexibly intertwine work and family

2. How to make baby-friendly adjustments to your budget

3. Relatively painless ways to transition from independent adult to responsible family member, which includes thinking about some difficult topics

THE NEW MOMMY (AND DADDY) TRACK

At 5:30 p.m. on a Tuesday, Lindsay Kelly wraps up the day at her law firm by printing out a stack of papers to work on at home. Photos of her husband and two-year-old son decorate her spacious office, which is otherwise filled with legal textbooks. Her soon-to-be-born daughter, scheduled for delivery in just a few days, is causing her belly to extend out from her otherwise thin frame. Lindsay has already been up for thirteen hours: she usually starts working before dawn so she can bill at least forty-five hours a week.

Lindsay, who's in her early thirties, originally decided to work at this particular law firm, based in Washington, DC, partly because of the flexible work arrangements it offered. "As long as you get everything done and meet the clients' needs, you can work whatever time of day you like," she says, as we walk through the summer rain to her nearby two-bedroom apartment.

As soon as we get in the door, her son calls out to her. "Mommy, Mommy, I went to the park!" As Lindsay unloads her papers and laptop from her shoulders, she listens to her son, George, and talks with Lysette, his nanny, about the day's adventures. After saying good-bye to Lysette, she slides pork tenderloin into the oven and pulls out prepared pasta salad from the fridge. Ready-to-eat meals from Whole Foods, along with takeout on nights she works late, make dinners relatively easy. Soon, her husband, a real estate developer also named George, gets home and starts playing with the younger George and his train set. Two-year-old George demands that his father pretend to be Sir Topham Hatt; big George obliges.

As dinner cooks, Lindsay goes into the den that serves as her office and her husband gives George a bath. When she logs onto her computer, she taps into her firm's network and has access to the same screen she sees from work. As she checks email and goes over paperwork, she takes a moment to reflect on her situation. "I enjoy working," she says, adding that she never thought of staying home after having children. Does she worry about what the law firm's partners and her colleagues think of her arrangement? "I'm certain there are people who don't like it, but I can't spend time worrying about it," she says. On the occasions that she's had to tell coworkers that she needs to go home in the middle of a meeting, she just briefly explains that she has to get home and then leaves. "Someone who has trouble asserting themselves would have difficulty," Lindsay acknowledges. "You have to set your own boundaries." But she knows that as long as she's billing her hours and doing a good job for her clients, then "it really doesn't matter where I'm sitting." With that, two-year-old George, fresh from his bath, climbs onto her lap.

In many ways, Lindsay is lucky. She has a job that allows her to work from home, a partner who shares many of the domestic responsibilities, and a household income that makes it possible to hire a full-time nanny. But increasingly, Lindsay's situation, or a variation of it, is becoming the norm instead of the exception. More parents are negotiating flexible arrangements, choosing to work for themselves, or simply deciding to work less in order to spend more time with their children.

✓ Quick Tip: Head Start

It's never too early to start teaching your children about money. Money Savvy Generation, a company that promotes financial literacy for kids, suggests giving children a piggy bank divided into four compartments, for saving, spending, donating, and investing. "You're teaching them to stop, pause, and reflect, and this is the first step toward teaching them to delay gratification," says company cofounder Susan Beacham. She also suggests sitting down as a family and drawing pictures of your goals, whether they include a vacation to the tropics or a new family pet, to help kids understand the rewards of saving.

The first step toward negotiating a flexible arrangement at work is to establish yourself as a productive and irreplaceable worker. The more specialized your skills (and usually, the higher your pay), then the more negotiating power you have. It can also help if you wait until you've established yourself as a valuable worker before trying to work out a flexible schedule. *The 4-Hour Workweek* author Tim Ferriss suggests first volunteering to work two Saturdays from home, and documenting your achievements during that time. Showing that having fewer interruptions and more autonomy leads to greater productivity can make a boss more amenable to working-from-home arrangements. Next, Ferris recommends proposing that you work from home on a Tuesday, Wednesday, or Thursday. (Mondays and Fridays look suspiciously like three-day weekends.) As your boss becomes more comfortable with the arrangement, then you may be able to work out even more flexibility.

Colleagues who already regularly work from home may be willing to share their advice and proposals. (The website workoptions.com also offers templates for flexible arrangements.) Ideally, the pursuit of flexibility begins during the job-hunting process. Before accepting your next job, try to find out how flexible the office is by talking to current employees about it. How often do people work at home? Is it encouraged? What are the typical hours spent in the office? How frequent is weekend work?

The Bureau of Labor Statistics reports that just over one in four parents with children under the age of eighteen works a flexible schedule[2]—but many workplaces still resist the idea. During economic downturns, when employees are grateful to hold on to their jobs, offices tend to scale back such perks, since they can afford to be more rigid.

The challenge of finding high-quality, affordable child care can seem insurmountable. It can seem even more impossible after the day-care center that was more than happy to take your $100 to add you to its waiting list informs you that because of an influx of siblings your child probably won't be welcome. And more so when you're dealing with nanny agencies, which often come with a $2,000 finder's fee.

Luckily, there are some less traditional options. (Regardless of the arrangement you choose, be sure to check to see if you are eligible for the child and dependent care tax credit, which can be as much as $1,050 per child. While the credit is lower for higher earners, it never phases out completely.)

- **Find your child-care provider online.** New websites, including the leading sittercity.com, have sprung up to help parents jump over the traditionally high-fee nanny agencies. For a membership cost of around $40, parents can search through over a million nanny and babysitter profiles, which include photos, references, and background checks. Parents can then interview the caregivers they're interested in themselves. "It puts the parents in the driver seat," says founder Genevieve Thiers. You can also use the site to look up average rates in your area to make sure you are not overpaying (or underpaying) your caregiver. (You also want to be sure to pay the appropriate taxes and verify employees' eligibility to work in the United States as described in chapter 7, page 116.)

- **Consider "hybrid care."** When the economy is in a slump, there tends to be more competition among caregivers, which means that not only are many willing to lower their rates but they may make themselves more appealing to employers by offering to do more than just child care. Light housework, dinner preparation, and even tutoring can come with the job, which means you might be able to save yourself time and money in other areas of your budget.

- **Trade services with other parents.** If you work part-time or stagger work schedules with your partner so you need only partial child care, consider trading services with other parents. Perhaps you can take care of your child and your neighbor's child from 9 a.m. to 12 p.m., and then hand them both over to the same neighbor from noon to 3 p.m., while you work.

- **Hire a caregiver with another family.** In this arrangement, often called a "nanny-share," parents can go in on one nanny together and split the costs. While sharing can be less convenient because it will likely involve some additional logistical and transportation arrangements, it can cut your costs almost in half. Just be sure that you agree with the other family on policies surrounding discipline, diet, and television watching for your children.

- **Form a co-op.** Also best for part-time workers or parents who want help during off hours, a babysitting co-op is made up of a group of parents (usually six or more) who take turns caring for each other's children. Parents earn points for each hour they babysit, and then they spend those points by "buying" child care for their own children. "It's a wonderful alternative to paying hourly for an occasional babysitter," says Lisa McLellan, a professional child-care provider and founder of babysittingworld.com.

- **Hire an au pair.** If you have space in your home for another resident, then hiring a young foreigner to handle child care while you're at work can be much more affordable than hiring a nanny. The U.S. State Department strictly regulates the au pair program, so you have to be sure to follow the rules: au pairs can't work more than forty-five hours a week and they can't take care of an infant younger than three months.

- **Find a stay-at-home parent who wants to take on another child.** Many stay-at-home parents have more than enough on their plates, but sometimes they're interested in earning extra money.

- **Look for local college students.** This approach also works best if you just need part-time child care, such as afternoons when college students tend to be done with classes for the day. By posting a help wanted ad on a local university job board, you can often find students to serve as babysitters for a few hours a day.

Because of the restrictions imposed by many workplaces, some parents decide to go into business for themselves. Rachel Thebault worked in investment banking throughout her twenties, but she knew she didn't want to keep up with the constant travel and long hours once she had children. "I felt like in the long term, that was not going to be a job where I felt like I could commit to being success- ful . . . and also happily raise a family," says Rachel, now thirty-four. Before becoming pregnant with her daughter, Marin, she left invest- ment banking and went to culinary school. Then, shortly after Marin was born, she opened a bakery, the popular Tribeca Treats in lower Manhattan. She still works long hours—as many as sixty to eighty a week—but because she's the boss she can spend the mornings with Marin, now four, and her second daughter, Sage, take them to doc- tors' appointments, and occasionally bring them to work.

In order to gain that freedom, though, Rachel has had to make some financial sacrifices. After giving up her six-figure salary in invest- ment banking, she and her husband, who works in finance, talked about how they could live on one income until her business got off the ground and she started paying herself a salary. "We both decided that ultimately, you couldn't put a price on my happiness. I'm a much different, more relaxed person now," she says. (She has since started earning money again, after getting a contract for her first cookbook.)

Annette Rubin, a thirty-nine-year-old resident of Seattle, Wash- ington, made a similar choice after returning to her position at Estée Lauder after the birth of her son, Jackson, now eight. She loved her job, but she hadn't found a caretaker she trusted to take care of him. The position also required a lot of travel, something she didn't want to do if she couldn't bring Jackson along. So she resigned and, with her husband, launched Belli Cosmetics, a skin-care line aimed at preg- nant women and mothers. While she was pregnant, she had noticed a lack of cosmetic products made for pregnant women, who often have concerns about ingredients and how they might affect the baby. Her husband, a doctor, contributes his medical expertise to the company.

Annette and her husband recently welcomed their second son, Cody, into the family. Even though she works forty to fifty hours a week, she organizes her schedule in order to maximize the time she spends with her sons. "It's worked out really well for our whole family," she says. After deciding to sell her company to Advanced Biotechnologies, she continues to serve as president, and she says she's never been more fulfilled. (As we saw in chapter 2, starting a business usually entails significant start-up costs and risks; having a financial cushion in place and maintaining a full-time job until profits start flowing can help ease the transition.)

Deciding to work less altogether is another option, as psychology professor Tim Kasser demonstrated earlier in this book. Research by Sylvia Ann Hewlett, author of *Choosing a Life: Professional Women and the Quest for Children*, found that more than one in three women temporarily stops working after having kids.[3] (Most of them would have preferred to work a job with reduced or flexible hours, if that choice had been available.) Indeed, a survey by the Pew Research Center found that almost two in three mothers now say that a part-time arrangement is ideal, compared to 48 percent in 1997. Only two in ten say their ideal is to work full-time; a similar percentage say they'd prefer to not work at all.[4]

While the discussion about work-life balance often centers on mothers, fathers are increasingly deciding that they should be the ones to scale back their work hours, at least temporarily, to care for their kids. That's what Jeremy Adam Smith, a forty-year-old San Francisco–based writer and editor, did after his son, now five, turned one. His wife was a full-time mom for the first year of their son's life, and then, when she was ready to go back to work, they switched roles. "My wife and I never assumed that one of us was the natural breadwinner and natural caregiver. Before my son was born, we assumed she would go back to work after six months, but she and he weren't ready, so she didn't work at all for the first year. Then, at a certain point, we talked about her going back, but we didn't want to put our son in day care. I wasn't sure we could afford it anyway. I was at a crossroads in my career. I could leave, and I did," he says. Jeremy, who had been working as a manager at a nonprofit, used the time to transition into full-time writing and editing. He worked for a few hours each morning before his wife left for work and his day with his son began. He ended up writing a book about his experience, *The Daddy Shift: How Stay-at-Home Dads, Breadwinning Moms, and Shared Parenting Are Transforming the American Family.*

☑ Quick Tip: Back to Work

Continuing to work, either on a freelance or consulting basis, while taking time out of the workforce can make it easier to return to a full-time career later. Writer Sharon Reed Abboud, author of *All Moms Work: Short-Term Career Strategies for Long-Range Success*, recommends maintaining networks, staying active in professional associations, following industry publications, and blogging on relevant topics. After she decided to stop working full-time as a business reporter, she continued to freelance and work as a career consultant after her youngest son started preschool. That made it easier for her to start up again as a full-time writer and editor when her kids got older.

According to the Census Bureau, there are some 140,000 stay-at-home dads in the United States, compared to 5.3 million stay-at-home moms.[5] But Jeremy argues that those numbers undercount stay-at-home dads, since they exclude fathers who do any paid work. He found that fathers are more likely to become the primary caregiver when the mother earns more or has better career prospects, and when fathers are able to take more parental leave from their jobs. Jeremy also found that the decision to rotate or share the caregiving role can boost a family's overall financial stability. He says, "There is no more lifelong employment. In that circumstance, families have to be nimble. They can't afford to specialize. Both parents have to be capable of taking on either of these roles. I think that's going to be the reality for a long time. You can resist that, or embrace it and understand what you're gaining. For women, they can gain a greater degree of personal independence and accomplishment in careers and jobs. For men, they can gain a fuller life and greater sense of humanity."

Combining full-time parenting with scaled-back work has become a way for both moms and dads to more easily transition back into the labor market when they're ready. Jeremy says, "In my experience, every dad on the playground did some work. One was a contract archeologist and went to Mexico once a month, another was a private chef and two nights a week would cook."

☑ Quick Tip: The Cost of Staying Home

When you're calculating how much leaving the workforce will cost your family, don't forget to include the value of future earnings and promotions. If child care costs about as much as your after-tax income, it might be tempting to think that you'll fare just as well financially by staying home. But that simple math doesn't take into consideration the fact that, over time, your child care costs will go down and your own salary will go up. Also, many parents find it difficult to find a job and transition back into the workforce after several years outside of it.

BABY BUDGETS

When I show up at Richelle Burnett's house midmorning on a Friday, her mother, who's visiting for the week, lets me in while Richelle finishes taking a shower and getting dressed. When she comes down, her stylish blonde hair still damp, she apologizes for running late; she got behind after walking her daughter to her group music lesson and then finding out it had been canceled. I'm there to witness the handover of an "Exersaucer," a bouncy chair that lets babies stretch their muscles. Her one-year-old son recently outgrew it, and she wants to turn it over to another mom on her neighborhood's listserv that makes this form of "freecycling," or getting used items for free, so convenient. Richelle originally got the chair from someone else on the listserv, and she now wants to pass it on to someone else who can use it.

Richelle's neighborhood is among Washington, DC's wealthiest; it's not where you'd most expect to find parents cutting corners to make ends meet. But Richelle, a working mom in her early forties, doesn't see the point of spending a lot on baby gear. If she can save money by picking up another family's discarded toys, why not? "I would rather be green and not have to buy something new," says Richelle, who estimates that her habit saves her at least $500 a year.

The days of mindlessly spending thousands of dollars in advance of bringing home a baby, and then thousands more on toys and other luxury items in the years that follow, are pretty much over, at least for anyone who doesn't want to participate in such excess. Parents are increasingly finding free or discounted items online, along with other ways of preserving their financial stability after having children.

☑ Quick Tip: Fighting Medical Expenses

Pregnancy- and newborn-related medical expenses quickly add up. If your insurance company ends up rejecting an expense, from a $600 sonogram to a $100 lab fee, don't forget to negotiate with your doctor's office. Asking for the discount normally given to insurance companies can cut your bill in half. (If you suspect the denial of coverage was in error, then follow up directly with your insurer.)

When Paul Golden, thirty-six, and his wife had their first child, they were shocked by the cost of child care. The Denver couple found themselves faced with a decision: should they continue maxing out their retirement savings, or did they need to put those monthly payments on hold while they raised their kids? They chose the latter option. Paul and his wife cut the amount they funneled into their

401(k)s while making sure to still save enough to earn their employer matches. (They plan to catch up later, after their now three- and six-year-old sons have outgrown the need for child care.) As soon as they get their retirement savings back on track, they will start saving for their sons' college costs. Paul estimates that even if they manage to soon begin putting away just $50 a month for each child, it would add up to about $15,000 each by the time they're college bound. "Personal retirement has to take precedence over college saving," says Paul, a spokesman for the National Endowment for Financial Education. While students can take out loans for college and have years to pay back the money, parents can't do the same for retirement—they need to have the cash in the bank before they stop working.

Jenny Ballman, a twenty-seven-year-old native of Shoreview, Minnesota, also found herself faced with a financial shock after having her first child, but for a different reason: she got laid off when she was seven months pregnant. "We hadn't really planned for it. I had counted on paid maternity leave and budgeted for me working the whole [nine months of pregnancy]," she says. She and her husband hadn't yet stored up any extra savings. In response to this unpleasant news, they cut all extras from their budget, including cable and dinners out. Then, as Jenny stocked up on baby gear, she looked for sales and used items. As her son got older, she learned how to make her own baby food. "It's always kind of stressful but we've done okay," she says. She doesn't feel like she's depriving her son of anything. She's also glad she didn't wait for a more stable job market to have her first child. "You could be waiting forever," she says.

Jae Jimenez, a twenty-something who works in sales, made a similar choice. He and his wife live with their ten-month-old daughter in a two-bedroom apartment in Brooklyn, New York, where he says they're happy. "We get so tired of hearing people say they have to live in a house once they get married or have a kid. Yes, it would be nice, but it's a luxury. . . . That's ridiculous to have such crazy expectations, especially right now," he says. He adds that his daughter doesn't notice the difference between living in an apartment and living in a luxury suburban home.

For writer Nan Mooney, the solution was more radical. In her late thirties, she decided to move across the country, from New York to Seattle, to live with her parents when she had her first child. "I wasn't financially ready, but my biological clock was ready," she says. She and her son now live in the lower level of her parents' townhouse and Nan is expecting her second child, who will join them in her parents' house. Her mom helps her with child care, which also generates big savings. Nan, the author of *(Not) Keeping Up with Our Parents*, has more time to spend with her son because she doesn't feel pressure to constantly work to earn more money. If she had stayed in New York, she says, "I would have needed a lot of public assistance. That's the only way I could imagine it working," she says. For single parents, who head about 9 percent of households, getting that additional support from family members can be especially important.[6]

☑ Quick Tip: Saving for College

Setting up a 529 college-savings plan is a great way to save for your child's future college education, because earnings are not taxed, as long as they go toward college tuition. To find the best one for you, compare the fees and investment options of different plans. Don't limit yourself to the ones offered through your own state; residency requirements generally only apply to prepaid tuition options. If you have an account at a brokerage firm such as Fidelity or Vanguard, you can start there. Fidelity, for example, manages 529 plans for California, Massachusetts, and a handful of other states. Some plans offer funds that automatically shift into more conservative investments as your child ages, but you want to be sure they are sufficiently conservative in order to protect yourself from any big downswings in the years leading up to high school graduation. If you want to have $200,000 saved for a child by the time he graduates from high school, then you need to save about $500 a month from his birth, assuming an average return of 6 percent.

When I first discovered I was pregnant, my husband and I thought we would need to move out of our one-bedroom apartment and into a two-bedroom rental or house before the baby was born. But, as we realized how expensive both those options would be, our one-bedroom started to look more appealing. When I asked a local online mom's forum, dcurbanmom.com, if I would go crazy living in such a small space with a baby, the overwhelming response was no. In fact, many moms said it was a pleasurable rite of passage. "Enjoy every crowded moment," recommended one poster, and dozens wrote to say that they had found a way to manage in small spaces, by using the trunks of their cars as temporary storage, setting up dividers, or just buying as little baby gear as possible.

☑ Quick Tip: Smaller Living

If you live in a small space, consider the "open-floor-plan nursery," the name my husband and I jokingly gave to our efforts to fit a new person into our one-bedroom apartment. The changing station and dresser fit next to our living room bookshelves, the swing hung by the kitchen table, and the cosleeper sat next to our bed. After all, open floor plans for kitchens are trendy, so why not for nurseries?

Downsizing one's vision of family life isn't for everyone. For Jennifer Rescigno, a recruiter in her late thirties in northwestern New Jersey, delaying, or even not having, children seems like the most responsible financial move. As a contract worker, she has periods when she is out of work, and her husband's job in retail doesn't generate enough income to support a family of three. "We would want to own a house before having kids," she says. Her husband, Lance, grew up in an apartment in New York, and it's important to him to give his kids space to run around outside, she reports. Jennifer also worries about the cost of health insurance and paying off credit card debt and student loans, as well as her current lack of maternity benefits. "I've never wanted to put a child in a position where we can't afford them," she says. For now, she and Lance have decided to wait before starting a family.

☑ Quick Tip: Are You Ready for a Baby?

While much of the decision to become a parent has nothing to do with money, getting financially ready can make life less stressful for your new family. Before plunging into parenthood, consider taking these steps:

- Wait until after the birth to purchase toys and gadgets (such as an Exersaucer) that aren't usually used until babies are several months old. You might find that your baby likes only certain kinds of toys, for example. By waiting, you will be sure that you are only buying things that you actually need.
- Borrow as much as possible from other parents, including used maternity clothes and baby gear. Your friends might be glad to put their items to good use.
- Sign up for your local community email group through free cycle.org or use craigslist.org to pick up used items from other parents in your area. Tips for finding discounts can also be found at babycheapskate.blogspot.com.
- Familiarize yourself with your workplace's maternity or paternity leave policies.
- Find out what it would cost to add an additional dependent to your health insurance.
- Before the baby arrives, save at least $10,000 for baby-related expenses during the first year.
- In addition, save enough money to fund maternity and paternity leaves as well as at least three months of living expenses in case of an unexpected job loss.
- Practice living on $1,000 less each month, which is the average cost of child care. Or, if either you or your spouse plans to stay home, practice living without that second income.
- Anticipate any major purchases, such as a new home or car, that you will need to make before welcoming home a new member of the family.
- Update (or create) your will and life insurance benefits.

Many couples make a similar decision. "Money is one of the reasons people are having children later," says Pamela Paul, author of *Parenting Inc.*, which explores the rising costs of child rearing. By Paul's estimates, the cost of raising kids has increased 66 percent over the last decade, while household income has risen by just 24 percent.[7] Many of those child-related costs, though, are unnecessary. Parents feel pressure to buy toys that supposedly stimulate their babies' brains, enroll in gym classes that are geared more toward parents than kids, and purchase electronic teddy bears to keep them company during time-outs.

Other baby costs can't be avoided. Health insurance, for example, helps pay for the many visits to the doctor's office that even healthy babies require. A premature or sick baby can easily cost tens of thousands of dollars during his first year. (Health insurance is also essential for moms; a standard birth can cost upwards of $10,000, and the fees are much higher for Caesarean sections.) And many moms want to take several months or more of maternity leave, which usually costs them most or all of their salaries for that period.

Another expense that becomes especially important after having children is also one of the hardest to talk about—life insurance.

TALKING ABOUT WHAT NO ONE WANTS TO TALK ABOUT

When Mark Colgan, a financial planner, was thirty, he discovered his wife, who was twenty-eight and had congenital heart disease, having a heart attack. Within hours, she was declared dead and the first responders were asking him where they should take her body for the autopsy. Not only did he not know what to tell them but he wasn't even sure how to begin to respond to the other questions suddenly facing him, from how to honor her legacy to how to plan the funeral.

Then, there were the endless logistical questions, such as what Mark should do with the bills that came addressed to her and what she wanted done with her belongings. "I was a certified financial planner, and even as an expert, I was overwhelmed," says Mark.

He realized that he wasn't the only one who had found himself totally unprepared for such an unexpected, tragic situation. So he wrote *The Survivor Assistance Handbook: A Guide for Financial Transition*, and founded Plan Your Legacy, a company that prepares financial advisers and attorneys to help people get ready for death, including how to leave a meaningful legacy. The book and accompanying online tool ask people to answer questions about their lives and values, such as how they want their children to be raised, how they define success, and their family history. It also includes details about where their money and financial paperwork is located, whether they have a life insurance policy, and if they've extended personal loans to relatives and friends. Even people who write wills and take out life insurance often fail to have those deeper conversations with family members, he says. But when survivors receive those details after the death of a loved one, "it's priceless," says Mark, who is now forty-one and lives with his second wife and their two young children in Pittsford, New York.

The challenge, explains Mark, is that people resist talking about inheritance and death. That's why he frames the discussion in terms of legacy, which encompasses family values, traditions, assets of emotional value, and money. If people don't talk about those subjects ahead of time, then not only do they lose out on learning their family members' preferences and thoughts on the subject but they may also be so consumed with heartache that they have difficulty making the best financial decisions.

The difficulty of broaching this subject explains why most Americans don't even have a will, and why many don't have enough life insurance. When I tried to persuade my husband—on the way to childbirth education class—that we should sign up for life insurance as soon as possible, he said, half jokingly, "What else do you want us to spend money on that doesn't get us anything?" In a way, he's right—the person who takes out life insurance will never see the benefits, other than the peace of mind that comes from knowing that his or her family will be protected from financial hardship in the event of death. (A few minutes after I brought up the subject of life insurance, I mentioned that I had also drafted our wills and printed them out. "You're just a barrel of laughs tonight," he said, before quickly changing the subject.) We signed up for life insurance a few weeks later.

☑ Quick Tip: Finding (and Being) a "Trusted Person"

If you're in charge of helping an older family member with his or her own finances, then you might want to consider adding your name to his or her accounts. When Catherine Collinson, president of the Transamerica Center for Retirement Studies, became her grandmother's "trusted person" after her grandfather passed away, they did just that. "It was painful for me. I said, 'Nothing will happen,' and she replied, 'At age eighty-nine, something might happen.'" Her grandmother explained to Catherine the details of her accounts, insurance, and preferences about assisted living facilities, and then they visited all of her banks to add Catherine's name to the accounts. That way, Catherine could pay the bills if her grandmother became incapacitated. Then, when her grandmother had a severe stroke at age ninety-two, Catherine was able to easily take control. "I could jump in instantly and take care of things. I could talk to the insurance companies and Medicare. I would never have been able to represent her otherwise," says Catherine.

Although the chance of tragedy is extremely low, ignoring the subject of life insurance and wills can cause unnecessary stress during a time of grief, and it can cause your loved ones financial hardship in the event of such an unlikely occurrence. And, because of the low risk of death among twenty-, thirty-, and forty-somethings, we can lock in attractive rates. If you take out a policy now, you can guarantee yourself relatively low annual payments for the next ten, twenty, or thirty years. If you decide to take out more life insurance later, your new rates will be pricier because you're older, but you can augment the relatively cheap coverage you already have, and this solution will end up being less expensive than taking out a brand new policy.

So, what do you need to do? First, the basics: do you know where your money is, how much there is, and how to access it? Amid typical chore delegation and specialization within marriage, one person often heads up the finance department. That can be helpful, as long as the other person has at least a working knowledge of the details, in case he suddenly needs to take over one day. In fact, a study by the Hartford Financial Services Group and MIT AgeLab found that the most financially successful couples are the ones who divide up financial tasks so they each do some of them.[8] For example, one person might pay the bills while the other handles investments. Those couples were more likely to save more and have a financial plan in place in the event of one person's death than couples where one person handled all the money management. But only about one in ten couples share the reins this way.

Given the statistics that women are far more likely to be widowed one day than vice versa, it's especially important for women to make sure they stay on top of their family's finances. By some estimates, 80 to 90 percent of women will have to manage their finances on their own at some point in their lives, because of either death or divorce.

☑ Quick Tip: Divorce Economics

As long as you were married for ten or more years, then you're entitled to an ex-spouse's Social Security benefits if they exceed your own. If you want any part of your ex-spouse's 401(k) or life insurance policy, then you need to negotiate that into the divorce settlement. Widows and widowers are also able to receive their spouses' Social Security benefits.

Second, do you have enough life insurance? Chances are that your workplace benefits, if you have any, aren't enough. But the right amount isn't necessarily obvious. The standard rule about having seven to ten times annual income doesn't make much sense for a single thirty-year-old with no kids, but it might not be nearly sufficient for a father of two with a stay-at-home wife. To calculate the amount that makes sense for you, you can either figure out what it would cost to replace your income, or add up all of the expenses you'd like to be able to pay for in the event of your death. For example, would you want to pay off your mortgage? Pay for your kids' educations? If you're a stay-at-home spouse, would you want your partner to be able to hire a full-time caregiver for your kids? The figure you arrive at might scare you; it could easily be over $1 million. But even if that's the size of the policy you decide to get, it's unlikely to break the bank. Term insurance, which covers a certain time period, typically ten to thirty years, is usually much more affordable than permanent life insurance, which also acts as an estate planning tool, and you can usually lock in low rates for term coverage that last up to thirty years. A $1 million term insurance policy for a healthy thirty-year-old might cost around $800 a year. If that's too much, settle on a figure that your budget can handle. You can always add coverage later.

Once you decide on an amount, you can quickly compare various insurers' costs by visiting their websites and getting a quote. You can also contact a broker, or use a comparison website such as intelliquote.com, which can find the cheapest policy for you. Unless the insurer is a major bank that you're already familiar with, it's worth researching the company to make sure it's sound and legitimate. After you select the plan that makes the most sense for you, the insurer will likely schedule a health checkup at your home before offering you the policy.

Q. If my insurer goes bankrupt, does my life insurance policy still exist?

A. Before signing up with an insurer, do some background research on its stability. Various firms rate insurance companies based on their likelihood of suffering from financial problems, and you want to pick one that looks secure. But sometimes, as happened with AIG in 2009, a giant insurer quickly goes from being an apparent pillar of financial security to needing government support. The good news is that, if an insurer suddenly becomes insolvent, state guarantee associations step in. By law, every insurance company must pay into these associations, which makes sure policies are honored in the event of bankruptcy. But customers aren't guaranteed 100 percent of their benefits in the event of such insolvency. The specific rules vary by state, but associations typically guarantee up to $300,000 in death benefits, for example.

Another topic that suddenly becomes relevant when you have dependents is a will. At its simplest, a will just describes who will be responsible for your assets and children if you die. If your situation involves children from previous marriages or significant assets, you will want to work with a lawyer. But if your responsibilities are limited to a home and a baby, then you can probably write a will the easy way—online. Several websites, including buildawill.com and legacywriter.com, offer standard will templates for around $20. You just need to fill in the blanks. If you have a spouse or partner, then you can create duplicate wills so they don't contradict each other. The requirements for executing the will vary by state, but you will likely need to sign the documents in the presence of at least two other people.

Once you have your will and life insurance taken care of, you can put them in a safe place in your home and also send copies to one or two people you trust, such as the person you select as the executor of your estate. That way, they know where to find the information if they need it. They should also know where to find information about the location of your assets and financial accounts. In addition, you want to make sure your spouse knows where to find all of the passwords to any joint as well as individual accounts.

☑ Quick Tip: Special Needs, Special Planning

When kids have special needs, such as autism or Down syndrome, and require financial support throughout their lives, parents need to prepare well in advance. The government, through Medicaid and Social Security, usually covers basic medical care, but recipients of that care can become ineligible if they hold assets over $2,000. Parents can avoid that cap by setting up special needs trusts, where all their child's assets, including any that will be inherited, can be directed. Karen Greenberg, mother of a son with autism and director of Prosperity Life Planning (prosperitylifeplanning.org), a nonprofit that teaches financial planning to families of children with special needs, says that "survivorship" or "second to die" insurance policies can be useful because they pay out only after the second person dies and are usually more affordable than individual life insurance policies. Greenberg recommends using them on top of any additional life insurance policies parents take out for other estate-planning reasons.

Greenberg created a special-needs trust for her son, Ricky, now in his early twenties, when he was six years old, by putting $400 a month into it. With half of that accumulated money, she bought a survivorship policy with a death benefit of $650,000 and invested the rest in mutual funds. Now, the investment has grown enough that she can use the income it generates to pay for the life insurance premiums.

With that taken care of, you can get back to happier topics, like whether baby sign language classes are really for you or maybe even whether you're ready to think about affording baby number two. After our archetypal couple Kenneth and Danielle had their first child, Sophia, they decided to split up their child-care duties for the first four months: Danielle took three months of maternity leave from her job, and then Kenneth used his paternity leave for the fourth month. By the time Sophia was five months old, they had found another family also interested in a nanny-share arrangement and began dropping Sophia off there each day.

Despite their relatively smooth transition, their budget faces many more constraints than it did before: instead of saving a few thousand dollars each month, they're lucky if they can squeeze a few hundred into their money market fund. That bothers Kenneth, who has always preferred saving to spending. They still have a healthy emergency savings fund in case one of them loses a job, but since they're considering moving into a three-bedroom home, they may have to give up that cushion to have enough cash for a down payment. For now, though, they're holding off, mostly because they don't want to take that kind of risk—especially with the local commercial real estate market drying up a bit, making Danielle's architecture job less secure than it was a few years ago.

Plus, Kenneth and Danielle are considering getting another one of their dreams off the ground soon. Ever since their engagement trip, they've been drawn to the fight against poverty in Ecuador. They've considered donating food or money, volunteering their services on their next vacation, or setting up some kind of microlending program so their friends and family members could help get a handful of Ecuadorians' small businesses off the ground. Kenneth is also growing increasingly frustrated with the long-term prospects for his consulting job, which often requires sixty-hour workweeks and leaves him little time to spend with Sophia. He wonders if his passion for helping entrepreneurs in developing countries could turn into a second career. That question—how to incorporate changing the world into the rest of their financial lives—is one that a lot of young professionals are asking themselves.

Exercises: Supporting a Family

1. If you're considering expanding your family, then brainstorm about all of the child-related costs you're likely to encounter, from a monthly diaper bill that runs almost as much as the cable TV statement to the temporary (or permanent) loss of one family member's salary. After adding up the monthly costs, see if you can adjust your budget to make room for them. What would you have to give up, if anything?

2. Are you happy with your current work-family arrangement? Do you wish you could spend more or less time doing either? Consider proposing a flexible arrangement that would allow you to work at home on a regular basis, by emphasizing the ways it would increase your productivity.

3. Take a look at your child-related purchases. Are there more items you could pick up by searching local online forums or craigslist.org? Do you have clothes and toys that you could give away or sell, and free up some space around your house?

4. Calculate whether or not you have enough life insurance. Make a list of all of the expenses you would like to pay for in the event of your death, from supporting your family's current lifestyle to funding college tuition. Don't forget about health insurance and other benefits provided by your job. Inflation should also be factored in to the estimate. How does that number compare to the life insurance you actually have? If it falls short, visit a few insurers online to see how much it would cost to increase your coverage.

5. If you haven't done so already, write a will. If your assets and responsibilities are relatively straightforward, then writing a will through a website such as buildawill.com or legacywriter.com can take less than half an hour.

Part 3

CHANGING THE WORLD

10

GREEN SPENDING

The lure of organics can be tempting: the promise that you're supporting sustainable agriculture, in addition to avoiding certain chemicals, is almost as appealing as the products themselves. But can spending money on so-called "green" items really benefit the earth? Aren't we still generating waste, and maybe even more of it, especially if our organic strawberries were flown in from Brazil, or our eco-vacation involves traveling halfway across the world?

In this chapter, you'll learn the following:

1. When to spend more to go green, when to save your money, and how to avoid needing to make that choice

2. How to spot companies that are just pretending to be environmentally friendly

3. When to let your morals influence investing decisions

GREENING YOUR SHOPPING SPREE

Early on a Saturday morning, environmentalist Diane MacEachern is in her garden, cutting flowers to bring inside. I've asked her to show me how she built her environmentally friendly home. It's nestled in the shade between giant oak trees in the artsy neighborhood of Takoma Park, Maryland, where speed bumps stop cars from going more than five miles per hour and neighbors hang Tibetan flags on their porches.

Diane, author of *Big Green Purse* and force behind the popular website of the same name (biggreenpurse.com), starts with where we're standing. When she and her husband first built their home in the mid-1980s, they protected the roots of the trees now towering over us by erecting the house on stilts made out of old telephone poles. That way, there was no need to use tractors to dig up a big plot of land, which often kills the surrounding trees. That means that the red and white wooden house, which reminds me of the rickety beachfront hotel in *Nights in Rodanthe*, sits entirely above ground. As we climb the steps up to the wraparound deck, I feel a few mosquitoes nipping at my legs. With the yard full of native plants and trees, it feels more like we're in a national park than on the edge of Washington, DC. The shade also keeps the home cool in the muggy summers, reducing the need for air-conditioning.

Natural light comes through the big living room windows, illuminating peach walls, so Diane doesn't need to turn on any lights for us as she points out the home's other green features. (Those windows also let the house warm up naturally during the winter, so the family can often leave the heat off during the day.) The hardwood floors are made out of Brazilian cherry wood approved by the Forest Steward-ship Council for sustainability. The off-white carpet leading up to the second floor, where her two college-age kids are still sleeping, comes from recycled soda bottles, although it feels just like your typical poly-ester blend. Instead of buying new furniture when she and her husband renovated the house a few years ago, they reupholstered the thirty-year-old pieces they had. With the blue sofas draped with a colorful red blanket, they look like something you might see on display at Macy's. And when Diane cleans the house later today, she'll stick mainly with baking soda, vinegar, lemon, and water.

✓ Quick Tip: Green Preening

Jennifer Taggart, author of *Smart Mama's Green Guide*, recommends looking closely at the ingredients on personal hygiene products, including shampoos and perfumes. She avoids synthetic fragrances, which usually contain phthalates, a substance that has been linked to hormone disruption. But that doesn't mean she can't smell good. In fact, her approach allows her to pamper herself with fragrant products while also avoiding toxins and saving money. She makes her own body scrub by mixing sea salts in a coffee grinder and adding essential oils such as lavender or sweet orange oil. She makes perfume by heating together beeswax, oil (such as olive or almond), distilled water, and essential oils. If you want to check out the toxins that are in your store-bought products (and perhaps be inspired to cook up homemade versions), visit cosmeticsdatabase.com. Since it's easy to spend hundreds of dollars a year on perfume, body scrub, and other products, making your own after you invest in a handful of start-up ingredients— can also be a smart financial choice.

So, how much does all this sustainability cost? Diane and her husband paid about $1,500 extra for the certified wood and $600 extra for the peach paint, which is free of volatile organic compounds, or VOCs. But overall, the choices saved them money. Since the paint didn't emit any noxious fumes, the family was able to stay in the house during the renovation instead of moving into a hotel. Reupholstering the furniture, which Diane had done professionally, saved them a couple thousand dollars since they didn't have to buy any new pieces. The recycled-plastic carpet came from the national megachain Empire

Today and was the lowest-priced option. And her simple cleaning supplies are cheaper than bottles of store-brand chemicals.

As Diane's experience shows, "going green" often coincides with saving money. Dozens of other choices also benefit both the earth and budgets, including these possibilities:

- **Using less energy.** Small changes, like closing doors to unused rooms or turning off the air-conditioning during the day, can make a serious dent in utility bills. So can unplugging appliances, turning off lights, and shutting down computers at night. Even televisions can use up power when they're turned off, so unplugging them when they're not in use saves energy. A power strip known as the Smart Strip automatically cuts power to devices that don't need it when they're off, such as a DVD player, while maintaining power to those that do, such as a cable box. That saves the typical family about $15 a year, which means the $30 strip pays for itself after two years.

- **Changing lightbulbs.** Substituting compact fluorescent lightbulbs for incandescent bulbs will save around $30 per lightbulb and pays for itself after six months, according to the Energy Department.[1] New developments have made compact fluorescent lights more similar to natural lighting than they were previously.

- **Using fewer products.** Instead of lathering up with soap, shaving cream, shower gel, and body scrub, Diane MacEachern suggests cutting back to just a handful of products. "Put everything you use in one day on the counter and it will blow your mind. Pick a day where you just brush your teeth and your hair and forget about the rest," she says. In addition to creating less waste, the change will lower your monthly drugstore bills, because you won't be buying all of those unnecessary lotions and creams.

- **Making cleaning supplies from scratch.** Even Martha Stewart endorses this technique. A bowl of vinegar or simmering lemon rinds can absorb smells just as well as manufactured air freshener. Scrubs made out of baking soda and water make kitchens sparkle just like chemical-laden cleaners. The Internet contains hundreds of do-it-yourself recipes; Jennifer Taggart's thesmartmama.com can get you started.

- **Driving smarter.** Emptying the trunk of anything heavy, from camping gear to books you plan to donate, allows a car to use less gas, as does driving smoothly, without a lot of acceleration and deceleration. There's also the obvious trick: visiting the mechanic regularly to replace clogged air filters, tune up the engine, and make sure tires are properly inflated.

- **Renovating with recycled products.** The idea of installing someone else's used kitchen cabinets might sound extreme, and even a little dirty, but with a few of those DIY cleaning products you just learned to make, along with a new coat of VOC-free paint, used cabinets can actually result in a beautiful new kitchen. Habitat for Humanity's "ReStores" sell surplus materials at a steep discount. (Sales go toward funding more homes for low-income families.) Web searches for "architectural salvage" can also turn up gently used pieces, since some new home owners end up redoing the kitchens of just-built homes.

- **Canceling catalog subscriptions.** The website catalogchoice.com lets retailers know which customers no longer want to receive their mail. Participating companies agree to stop sending any more catalogs within three months. Signing up with 41pounds.org halts junk mail. The Direct Marketing Association (the-dma.org) will let its members know when people tell it they don't want to receive any more direct-mail marketing offers. Junk mail piles up over time, so these fixes can really make a difference in the long run. The Environmental Protection Agency estimates that we receive four million tons of junk mail each year, almost half of which is never even opened.[2] In addition to saving paper, you'll also prevent yourself from spending needlessly by avoiding the temptation of those glossy pages.

- **Making toilets more efficient.** Low-flow toilets use less water each time they're flushed. A traditional toilet can be transformed into a low-flow one by placing a soda bottle filled with sand or water in the tank. You'll lower your water bill, too.

- **Making other green home improvements.** The federal government offers incentives for home owners to install energy-efficient roofs, windows, heating and cooling systems, and other technologies in their home. Of course, many of these installations are pretty pricey, but the energy savings over time plus the tax incentives can make the investment worthwhile from a financial perspective, in addition to the environmental one. If you bought new energy-saving insulation for your home before the end of 2010, for example, you could have received a tax credit for 30 percent of the cost, up to $1,500. The available tax credits are constantly changing; the latest can be found on the Energy Department's Energy Star website (energystar.gov).

But sometimes, it does cost more to go green, and we have to decide whether the benefits justify the extra money. Organic food, which can cost up to twice as much as you'd pay otherwise, is one of those pricier options. Partly because of the wish to avoid pesticides, and also because of evidence that suggests organic food is more nutritious, many people—three in four Americans—happily swallow the additional cost, at least on occasion.[3] The Organic Center, a nonprofit that promotes scientific information on organics, published one comparison that found that 61 percent of the time organic products contain higher nutritional values than their nonorganic counterparts.[4] As for pesticide content in conventionally grown produce, fruits and vegetables with fragile skins, such as nectarines, peaches, strawberries, and sweet bell peppers, are most likely to contain higher levels, while those with hard husks or rinds, such as corn or mango, come with more natural protection.[5] The new evidence has led Whole Foods, which has traditionally been cautious about making the organic-nutrition link, to become a bit bolder on the subject. "Our position on that is moving in the direction of organic food being more nutritious. . . . We're very optimistic based on a number of studies," says Joe Dickson, the company's quality standards coordinator. If the organic-nutrition link does prove true, then deciding to spend more money on organic food makes as much sense as other preventive health measures, such as paying for a gym membership or a bottle of vitamins. In the long run, if such moves help you avoid illness, then they will also save you a lot of money (in addition to maintaining your ability to work and earn income).

Along with improving your health, paying extra for organic food can also be better for the earth. To use the organic label, which is regulated by the USDA, food producers must avoid most traditional pesticides, petroleum-based fertilizers, and antibiotics, as well as growth hormones for animals. They also have to avoid using sewage sludge (as fertilizer) and genetic engineering. Locally grown produce also often costs more because it tends to be grown on smaller farms, but it likewise benefits the earth by reducing carbon emissions. In fact, many environmentalists prefer to buy locally than organically, if forced to make that choice.

A cheaper alternative to going organic involves shifting to a more vegetarian diet, which can also reduce your carbon footprint. A University of Chicago study found that consuming around 20 percent of one's calories from animal products generates about as much greenhouse gas as driving a typical sedan instead of a Prius. Someone consuming around one-third of his or her calories from red meat is responsible for about as much greenhouse gas as would result from driving an SUV instead of a sedan. (Greenhouse emissions come from using energy to run farms as well as the methane and nitrous oxide emissions from animals.) In other words, you can do as much good for the earth by avoiding meat as you can by driving around in a fuel-efficient hybrid car.[6]

☑ Quick Tip: Where Clothes Come From

The label on your polo shirt that says it was made in Indonesia doesn't tell you much about the conditions under which it was made. Were the workers paid a living wage? Did they have to work longer than eight hours a day? Were they children? Sometimes you can get more information by visiting a company's website and reading about their sourcing. You can also look up reports on retailers' factory conditions at the Fair Labor Association (fairlabor .org), which monitors conditions worldwide.

If that doesn't give you the information you want, then follow the advice of Kelsey Timmerman, author of *Where Am I Wearing: A Global Tour to the Countries, Factories and People That Make Our Clothes*, who recommends calling the company in question and asking to speak to the director of corporate social responsibility or the person in charge of sourcing. That way, you'll know more about the impact your spending is having on the larger world. If you're as adventurous as Kelsey, then you can combine your next vacation with a visit to the factory that made your jeans.

Because so many people are interested in going green, by buying organic food, or avoiding chemicals in cleaning products, it's getting easier and cheaper to do so. Growing consumer pressure is a big reason why we can buy organic baby food at Walmart and find vegetarian options on most takeout menus. After the outcry over BPA, or bisphenol A, in baby bottles and other plastic products, the six biggest makers of baby bottles stopped using the chemical altogether.[7]

Now that more consumers demand VOC-free paint, you can find it at Home Depot and Lowes. And Clorox released its line of natural cleaners in early 2008 to compete with Seventh Generation and other all-natural brands. When used effectively, our wallets hold a lot of power.

✓ Quick Tip: Blog Power

If you write a blog, especially a popular one, then you have another way of influencing company behavior: write about it. When Diane MacEachern and her fellow participants in the Green Moms Carnival started blogging about toxic chemicals found in Johnson & Johnson baby products, the company got in touch and started talking to the mothers about steps it was taking to address the situation. Even small blogs can catch the eye of corporations, which often receive automatic alerts that let them know when their company name is mentioned online. To expand your reach, team up with other bloggers who write on similar topics. Linking to each other's stories and letting media outlets know when you're onto something newsworthy will make companies more likely to pay attention.

Sometimes, though, companies are just faking it, and falsely advertising themselves as green, a problem known as "greenwashing." Claiming a "green" connection is understandably tempting; many companies would like to cash in on the $600 billion–plus marketplace for such products.[8] After examining over 2,000 products, TerraChoice, an environmental marketing firm, found that 98 percent of them came with advertising materials that made at least one misleading or false environmental claim. For the most part, labels that say things like "all-natural" or "green" don't mean much.[9] Green home design consultant Maggie Wood says she often comes across products touted as sustainable just because they contain a small amount of recycled content. One of her clients wanted to use a countertop that came with glossy literature boasting about its recycled content and sustainability. But, after investigating, Wood found it was made of just 10 percent recycled content and had no other green attributes. "It was imported from China, which isn't green because of the shipping involved. All the other materials were just virgin products and you couldn't recycle it at the end of its life," she says. Looking for third-party approvals, such as the Green Seal, can help you separate legitimate environmental friendliness from the fakers, as can Internet searches of products and ingredients. (Emailing the company directly when answers prove elusive is another option.) In many cases, companies charge a premium for green products, so you want to make sure you get your money's worth.

☑ Quick Tip: Eco-Friendly Luxury?

The new trend in global luxe travel is green: resorts on the islands of Thailand as well as game reserves in South Africa promise "green" getaways in the form of organic dining, local nature trips, and carbon offsets. But how green can these vacations be when they require a fourteen-hour trip on a jumbo jet to get there?

It's all in the details. Some of these resorts are about as green as John Edwards's megamansion in North Carolina. But others have a legitimate claim to the sustainable label. One eco-tour operator in Jackson Hole, Wyoming, in partnership with the nonprofit carbonfund.org, fuels its vehicles with biodiesel, uses only existing hiking trails in order to minimize the impact of visitors on the environment, uses washable lunch plates, and serves organic and local produce. Concerned travelers can also offset their carbon footprint further by funding wind energy, reforestation, and renewable energy projects through carbonfund.org.

The bottom line: if a vacation spot calls itself green, don't take its word for it. Since "green" vacations usually cost more, you want to make sure the designation is justified.

DO YOUR INVESTMENTS MATCH YOUR CONSCIENCE?

About fifteen years ago, when Cliff Feigenbaum was in his late twenties and working in the business office of a hospital, he discovered that his 401(k) plan was heavily invested in tobacco stocks. "I thought, 'This seems really inappropriate for a health care institution,'" he recalls. He spoke with the company's chief financial officer, who asked him to bring him information on other options—and to avoid mentioning his discovery to other employees, who might be similarly upset.

Shortly afterward, Cliff left his hospital job to start the Santa Fe–based *GreenMoney Journal*, which reports on the world of socially responsible investing and has more than 30,000 subscribers. He discovered he wasn't the only one with concerns. Today, companies increasingly offer socially responsible investing options through their 401(k)s. The Social Investment Forum, which represents the socially responsible investing, or SRI, professional community, estimates that $2.7 trillion out of the total $25.1 trillion U.S. investments, or about 11 percent, are socially responsible. That's an increase of about 18 percent since 2005.[10]

One challenge in understanding socially responsible investing, and how it works, is to define it. For some people, it means avoiding companies that sell alcohol or profit from gambling, while others might have no problem investing in a brewery but would never put their money into a military company. In general, SRI refers to four different strategies:

1. **Positive screening.** Investors select companies that reflect their values, such as those that pursue renewable energy projects or sell organic food.

2. **Negative screening.** People avoid investing in companies that conflict with their values. Traditionally, this process screens out tobacco, alcohol, gambling, and military companies.

3. **Community investing.** People put their money into low-income or otherwise underserved areas, including in developing countries.

4. **Shareholder activism.** Investors buy stocks in the companies that they hope to reform from the inside. For example, the Humane Society might purchase stock in McDonald's and then lobby for it to purchase only cage-free eggs.

☑ **Quick Tip: Getting Started with Socially Responsible Investing**

Chances are that your current brokerage house, whether it's Vanguard or Merrill Lynch, already offers socially responsible funds that have been screened for their environmental and social impact. If you don't currently use a broker but want to start investing in SRI funds, you can do it yourself through one of the big brokerage houses (such as Vanguard, which is known for low fees) or you can find a financial adviser familiar with SRI. The Social Investment Forum offers a directory on its website (socialinvest.org).

Ian McLeod, an investment adviser at the Berkeley-based Social Equity Group, which specializes in SRI, says that when a client first comes to him, he starts with a conversation about what it means to integrate values into an investing strategy. Sometimes, he says, people come in with such strict standards for what they don't want to invest in that they end up excluding most of the market. "You take on too much risk if you want to cut out 90 percent of companies," says Ian. He adds that, as is the case with all investing, it's important to look at the fund fees, which are sometimes higher than those of non-SRI funds because of their smaller size and the extra research involved.

If your only investments are through your 401(k) and you don't see any SRI offerings in your company's options, then you may have to ask your human resources department to consider adding one. Sometimes, Ian says, companies just haven't thought about it before and are happy to oblige.

Hundreds of academic studies have explored the question of whether SRI funds provide competitive returns. In general, the answer seems to be that they do, which is good news for socially responsible investors. Morningstar mutual fund analyst David Kathman says that any differences in performance are so small that they're not worth worrying about. He adds that SRI funds tend to be more heavily weighted with technology stocks and have fewer investments in manufacturing and industrial stocks because of environmental concerns. As a result, the funds tend to do well when the tech sector does well, and vice versa.

☑ Quick Tip: Sinful Investing

Sometimes, your conscience comes with a price. So-called "sin stocks," named because they invest in morally questionable industries, such as tobacco and alcohol, can hold up quite well during down markets. It's easy to figure out why: people tend to give up other luxuries, such as vacations and high-end retail, before they relinquish those addictive comforts. Defense and gambling companies also tend to be somewhat protected from large dips. So, if you want a truly diversified portfolio, you might want to consider investing in companies that you wouldn't otherwise support. Of course, if you're sticking with index funds, then you're probably already doing that without even thinking about it: the S&P 500 Index includes Altria, parent company of Philip Morris, as well as defense companies Raytheon and Lockheed Martin.

Barbara Krumsiek, president and chief executive of Calvert Investments, one of the biggest SRI investment management companies, argues that investing according to what she calls "sustainable" values coincides with better business. She told NPR that as an SRI investment manager she looks for the same qualities that lead to business success, such as diverse boards of directors, reasonable executive pay plans, and environmentally friendly products, which are increasingly popular with consumers.[11] That's one reason why she says many of Calvert's funds have beaten or performed on par with the market, especially throughout the financial crisis—Calvert largely avoided the financial institutions that were engaged in sub-prime lending and what some would consider predatory practices.

As for whether investing with your conscience is worth the extra effort it requires, for some investors it comes down to the fact that they don't want to go to bed at night knowing that they're making money off of bombs and cigarettes. Sometimes the impact of SRI investing is more concrete, such as when a company agrees to make its board of directors more diverse in response to a shareholder petition or a manufacturer agrees to reduce its carbon emissions. Stu Dalheim, Calvert's director of shareholder engagement, says that back in 2007 the investment company noticed that most major airlines were not making any sort of disclosure about their environmental practices. As a result, Calvert filed shareholder resolutions with United Airlines, US Airways, Continental, JetBlue, and Southwest. Every company except Southwest agreed to produce sustainability reports by 2008. At Southwest, the resolution instead came to a shareholder vote, which garnered enough support (26 percent of votes) to get the company's attention. And in 2009, Southwest agreed to produce a sustainability report. Those reports, explains Dalheim, encourage companies to adopt better environmental practices, since they bring greater attention to how they are responding to environmental concerns. Calvert also successfully petitioned for changes in corporate policy at American Express, Capital One, and dozens of other companies.

Cliff Feigenbaum gives at least partial credit for the publicity around excessive executive pay to SRI investors petitioning companies about it and bringing it up at shareholder meetings. "There's not a board in this country that hasn't had an executive compensation conversation in the last year," he says.

As with organic food and carpeting made from recycled materials, the value of socially responsible investing depends on a person's priorities. Even when it doesn't cost any money, it takes time and energy to seek out and research SRI funds. Our friend Kenneth couldn't care less about the subject, so he sticks strictly to the broadest index funds he can find, while his wife, Danielle, refuses to invest in oil and military companies. Her architecture firm offers an SRI index fund in its 401(k) plan, so she puts most of her retirement savings into that. And when it comes to buying food for their now one-year-old daughter, they both prefer to shop exclusively in the organic aisle.

Exercises: Sustainable Makeovers

1. Think about what you bought this week, including clothes, food, and personal hygiene products. Would buying organic have cost you more? Did you avoid extra packaging where you could? Do you know the conditions under which your clothes were made? Consider whether taking environmental and social justice factors into account would be worth it to you.

2. Is your home wasting energy? Check to see whether you tend to leave electronic equipment on when it's not in use, including computers and television paraphernalia, such as your Nintendo Wii and cable boxes. If turning them off is a pain, consider buying a power strip that automatically cuts power to accessories when they're not in use.

3. If you eat meat, consider swapping out a few meat-based meals for vegetarian ones each week.

4. Visit carbonfund.org to calculate your carbon footprint. What could you do to reduce, or offset, some of your carbon emissions, in a way that also saves you money? You might consider taking public transportation instead of driving, or reducing the number of airplane trips you take each year.

5. Look over your investments. Do you own stock in any companies, including companies in your index funds, that you don't like? Does your office's retirement plan offer any socially responsible options? If not, consider asking the human resources office to add some.

11

THE NEW RULES OF PHILANTHROPY

When young professionals want to give back, we tend to stay away from the big, established charitable foundations and instead pursue our own, more involved—and more social—paths. Some young professionals give 10 percent of their income to charity; others give $10 a month. Many combine volunteering with monetary gifts or donate items that don't cost anything, such as used clothes or books. We also increasingly pool our resources, through informal groups or more organized start-up nonprofits and giving circles, to leverage our limited philanthropy dollars.

In this chapter, you'll learn the following:

1. How to combine philanthropy with networking and socializing

2. How to evaluate which charities are worthy of your hard-earned cash

3. How to decide how generous you want to be

GLAMORIZED GIVING

As I enter the side door of the National Archives, an imposing build-ing that houses the Declaration of Independence and Bill of Rights, I feel a bit like Nicolas Cage sneaking around in *National Treasure*. It's after hours, and I can't shake the feeling that I'm doing something I shouldn't be as I slide through security, past some yellowed doc-uments (was that the Constitution?), and upstairs to a room full of people enjoying cocktails. Like the other young professionals sipping white wine and nibbling on cheese, I'm here for an evening discus-sion on politics with David Brooks of the *New York Times*, E. J. Dionne of the *Washington Post*, and historian Douglas Brinkley.

Since I don't see anyone I recognize, I make small talk with a group of people who have known each other since college and who all moved to Washington and work in a variety of corporate and govern-ment positions. Someone jokes about slamming back as many drinks from the open bar as possible before heading downstairs for our dis-cussion. Before we split up, one of my new friends gives me his card in case I ever want to write about his company.

This—an informal evening full of drinks, entertainment, and young people—is the new face of philanthropy. In this case, the good cause is the preservation of history. The Young Founders Society, the host of the event, meets about once a month to promote awareness of the National Archives and to raise money for the preservation of his-torical documents, as well as to enrich participants' own social and professional lives.

David Don, a thirty-nine-year-old lawyer, started the group to encourage other young professionals to appreciate and support the archives housed at the museum. With the help of a handful of friends, he worked with the National Archives Foundation's staff to decide on the group's goals and structure. They decided to set a relatively low price point—just $50 on top of membership levels that range from

$60 to a couple thousand dollars a year—in order to attract as many people as possible. "We decided it wasn't just about money. We also wanted to raise awareness of the institution," explains David.

The group has hosted evenings with Supreme Court justice Antonin Scalia, filmmaker Ken Burns, and other prominent politicians, journalists, and historians. Five years after it started, it has about seventy-five members and raises around $15,000 a year. The group also organizes joint happy hours with other young professional organizations in the area, such as those that support the Corcoran Gallery and Phillips Collection. "People come with friends, and meet other friends, and introduce each other. There's a significant amount of networking," says David. Whereas he could have achieved the same monetary impact by asking three of his friends to donate $5,000 a year instead of starting the group, it wouldn't have accomplished his other goals.

Not long after my evening at the archives, over on the other side of the country, another group of young people gathered for a different kind of charitable event. On a clear, mild Saturday night in Beverly Hills, the Society of Young Philanthropists' annual gala was just kicking off. The location—a private residence with a glistening green pool surrounded by bars stocked with Bacardi (one of the party's sponsors)—was kept secret until twenty-four hours prior as a security measure. As six hundred red-carpet-ready philanthropists in their twenties arrived, having paid about $200 each for a ticket, they were greeted with cocktails, a celebrity deejay, and a drummer who kept everyone moving until 2 a.m.

These entrepreneurs, marketing professionals, and otherwise well-to-do members of the Los Angeles glitterati were there for bigger things than making new friends and networking, although they were there for that, too. An amount of $20,000 from their ticket sales was headed toward two causes: Jenny McCarthy's Generation Rescue, which is dedicated to autism research and awareness, and Save a Child's Heart, an international organization that helps children get the cardiac care they need. The nearby tennis court was filled with photos of children who were alive because of Save a Child's Heart, and pamphlets and brief talks throughout the evening described the work of both organizations.

☑ Quick Tip: Form a Giving Circle

Join forces with friends by forming a giving circle, a group of people who pool their money to donate to a cause. The number of giving circles has doubled to at least eight hundred over the past four years, and the trend is partly frugality driven.[1] Combining money and time makes it easier to research charities more extensively, check up on how the funds are being used, and garner enough power as donors that charities make an effort to reach out to you. A representative might visit your donor circle one night to explain the programs, or invite you to participate in some of the charity's activities.

It's also a fun excuse to spend more time with your friends. Lisa Philp, forty-four, head of philanthropic services at J. P. Morgan Private Bank, helped create the Asian Women Giving Circle to support Asian American women-led projects and organizations that use the arts as a tool for social activism in New York City. Each of the circle's two dozen members raises at least $2,500 each year. Then, the group solicits proposals from potential grant recipients and later allows all contributors to vote on who will receive the money. In their first four years, they have given out over $270,000 to recipients ranging from the mentoring program Girls Write Now to Maria the Korean Bride, a performance artist who raises awareness about marriage pressures Korean Americans face. "You end up learning about more organizations than you would doing it on your own," says Lisa.

While her group is relatively formal and well organized, some giving circles keep themselves more low-key (and low-maintenance) by deciding on charities and then writing checks directly to that organization. But if the circle is big and you want to write a large group check, then you might want to consider setting up a non-profit structure so participants can write tax-deductible checks to the group before the funds are passed on to charities. To find a giving circle that already exists in your area, visit givingcircles.org.

The group started, as former board member Dana Corddry puts it, "with twenty-five kids in Beverly Hills." She explains, "It's common in this area to go to a friend's birthday party that's a fundraiser. Instead of accepting presents, she'll say, 'I'm turning twenty-five and am giving to this cause.' It's a fabulous party, they bring in great caterers. People love giving. Those have been some of the best parties I've ever been to." The Society of Young Philanthropists replicates that model on a much larger scale. So far, they've donated around $80,000 a year to charities and organize regular volunteer projects, from refurbishing wheelchairs for developing countries to taking foster kids to a baseball game.

Since members enjoy going to parties anyway, "we're just taking what we'd already be doing and making it useful," says Dana, twenty-nine. "People have the benefit of feeling good that they're giving to a cause, but part of the motivation is, 'I get to go out and hang out with my friends, have great entertainment, and have access to this network that will be helpful to me." That draw, she says, is part of the reason the group has swelled to over six thousand members in about five years. While most of them come from wealthy backgrounds, Dana says the group is becoming increasingly diverse.

On top of the do-gooding, the networking benefits of joining the Society shouldn't be underestimated. Since the group is made up of "trend-forward, professional young people of means" (Dana's words), they're well positioned to help each other out. Dana is currently launching her own event planning company, L'Artisan, and says she'll turn to her SYP contacts if she has trouble finding a vendor or is looking for a sponsorship. "Whether it's at executive board meetings, at parties, or while volunteering to plant trees on a Saturday . . . I've heard countless offers of assistance, shared contacts, and suggestions," she says.

Over the last several years, "shopping for a good cause" has become about as ubiquitous as those yellow "Live Strong" bracelets were in 2004. But is buying a pink ribbon or Save Darfur pin really going to make a difference? While the impact of your money depends on the organization receiving it, there are some basic rules of thumb to follow. Steer clear of sellers that make only vague claims. When a company promises that a "portion" of proceeds will go toward charity, you have no way of knowing how much, or how that money will be used. Even the Bono-supported Product Red campaign, which teamed up with retailers from Apple to the Gap to raise money for the Global Fund to Fight AIDS, Tuberculosis, and Malaria, fell under criticism for spending more on marketing than it raised for the fund.[2] Abusing a connection to charity is so common that a new word has been invented to describe it: pinkwashers. These are companies "who blatantly use support for breast cancer research" to promote their own reputation, according to Chicago-based ad agency Cramer-Krasselt.

A better bet is when the product lists a specific percentage along with the name of the charity on the receiving end. Sandra Miniutti of Charity Navigator, which rates charities, suggests avoiding products that you weren't planning on purchasing anyway. "It's not worth the time and the effort to buy a product just because it's affiliated with a charity. Usually the dollar figures are pretty small," she says. She adds that companies often have a limit on how much they give to charity, such as half a million dollars. If your purchase comes after that limit is reached, then it makes no difference at all for that charity.

If you still want to support a cause with your shopping habits, Sandra suggests visiting your charity of choice online and seeing if they have a store, which many do. Susan G. Komen for the Cure sells running gear directly on its site, and it specifies that 25 percent of the purchase price goes directly to the organization. As for those Live Strong bracelets, if you buy them from Lance Armstrong's official site, 100 percent of the proceeds go to the Lance Armstrong Foundation, which is dedicated to preventing and educating people about cancer. Other sellers, such as eBay, make no such promises.

The Young Founders Society in Washington and the Society for Young Philanthropists in Beverly Hills both exhibit traits that are unique to today's young givers, such as being directly involved in charities. "[Young people] are more hands on. You want to have a direct relationship with organizations and don't trust traditional non-profit structures as much," says Dwight Burlingame, associate executive director at the Center on Philanthropy at Indiana University. We also grew up at a time when volunteer work was often a high school graduation requirement, so we're used to getting our hands dirty.

Part of the reason for our direct participation is that we like to know that our dollars are actually making a difference. "It comes as a shock to Generation X to realize that older generations do so little to actually find out if what they're doing works. . . . Gen X is market-oriented. They came of age in an era of globalization," explains historian and generational expert Neil Howe. That's also why microlending programs, where donors lend small amounts of money to entrepreneurs in developing countries, have become so popular. The recipients report on their progress and eventually pay the money back, which in some cases allows them to receive a larger loan. That kind of incentive structure makes a lot of intuitive sense to our generation, Howe says.

As David Don and Dana Corddry both demonstrate, we also like to have a good time while we're being generous. Or, as Neil Howe puts it, "They like to use philanthropy as an excuse to socialize." By combining social activities with philanthropy, he explains, we don't have to disrupt our lives to start giving to a cause—we just incorporate it into the activities we want to be doing anyway, as Dana says.

In other words, while the average sixty-something might give $30 a week through his church collection box and then forget about it, the average thirty-something will meet up with friends at a wine bar after work to talk about how they can work with the local Humane Society to get thirty dogs adopted this year. And then they'll each put in $100 and spend a Saturday to get it done (and perhaps end up bringing home a new best friend, too).

If you're lucky enough to know that you'll have some money coming your way from parents or grandparents, consider talking to them about it in advance. Many families decide to pass money on to their kids and grandkids while they're still living, not only to avoid estate taxes, but also so they can talk about how they want the money spent and give some of it away together.

It might sound like as much of a challenge as deciding whether to vacation in Rome or Turks & Caicos, but navigating these kinds of intergenerational wealth transfers can be tricky, and it is a situation faced by a significant chunk of the population. The Government Accountability Office estimates that, on average, the wealthiest 10 percent of baby boomers own $3.2 million worth of assets—much of which they intend to eventually pass on to their kids.[3]

Resource Generation is a group that helps young people of wealth figure out how to wield it responsibly. Twenty-nine-year-old Michael Gast turned to the group to help him decide how to handle money he received as a gift from his grandmother. He had $40,000 left in the trust after paying for college and knew he wanted to give part of it away to social justice causes. "I wanted to align my relationship with that money to the values in the rest of my life—the values of economic justice and sharing resources—and I was really struggling with how to do that," he says. At a workshop hosted by Resource Generation, he learned how to create a giving plan that prioritized his values. A former educator, he now works full-time for Resource Generation as a family planning coordinator in Seattle.

Later, after Michael's grandmother passed away, he inherited an additional $50,000 and gives away 10 percent a year to charities. He's now talking with his brother, sister, cousins, parents, and other family members about coordinating their gifts through matching donations to further leverage the power of that inheritance. "I'm really inspired to continue developing these conversations with my family on how we could move these resources and make plans and share them with each other," he says.

CHOOSING WISELY

The first step toward becoming a philanthropist is to decide what really moves you. People find inspiration everywhere—books, movies, a conversation with a stranger, a glimpse of a war zone on the evening news. After watching the movie *Slumdog Millionaire*, I looked for an organization that helps Indian street children and ended up donating to the nonprofit my sister had volunteered for in Mysore.

Many people make the mistake of giving away small amounts of money throughout the year in response to requests from friends to support them in a breast cancer walk or multiple sclerosis awareness marathon. They never really connect to, or even choose, a single cause, which leaves them feeling like they're not supporting much of anything. It's often impossible to know if the gifts made any difference at all, or even where the money went. That's why it often makes more sense to focus on one or two causes instead, and to stick with them over time. A streamlined strategy also helps reduce junk mail—if you give a little to a lot of places, then you'll receive frequent requests for money, especially around the holidays. You might start to feel like the small amount you gave has been used up on mailing out more requests to you.

One method is to decide, usually at the beginning of the year, on your giving priorities. Perhaps you want to donate to your church's holiday food drive or give a certain amount of money per month to an international organization that fights poverty. Once you pick an area of focus, the next step is to learn as much as possible about it. If you believe passionately in addressing the world's water shortages, then you'll probably want to watch the documentary *Flow: For Love of Water* and check up on the United Nations' latest statistics on water shortages. You might even decide to plan your next vacation around a water hot spot, such as the Middle East, Sudan, or Nevada. Once you become something of a mini-expert, you will better know how to contribute. It might mean volunteering to dig irrigation ditches or buying a water tank for a family in India, or perhaps writing a letter to your representative in Congress, asking him or her to support better water management policies in dry states.

Megaphilanthropist Bill Gates told the *New York Times* in 2009, "The key thing is to pick a cause, whether it's crops or diseases or great high schools. . . . Pick one and get some more in-depth knowledge." He urged people to travel and see the problem in person when it's possible, and then to decide how to go about making a difference by supporting an organization with time or money.[4]

☑ Quick Tip: Give More, Get Happy

Doing good isn't the only reason to start being generous. It can actually make you a happier person, especially when you're feeling down about your own financial luck. Gretchen Rubin, author of *The Happiness Project*, says that when you give money away, you convince yourself that you're doing pretty well—well enough to give to others.

It also provides that elusive feeling of making a difference. "The thing people talked to me about over and over again was that their hearts and minds were open to finding something where they could give back, and each had a moment when they saw something they could no longer look away from," says Lisa Endlich, who profiled philanthropists in her book *Be the Change*. "This gave their lives a narrative, a meaning larger than themselves, the way parenthood does. . . . Their lives have been changed by changing other people's lives, and they have such profound gratitude that their lives are better," she says.

Of course, you also want to make sure your money isn't going to waste—or into keeping the air-conditioning running at some giant nonprofit's headquarters—and that it is going toward actually helping the cause that you've chosen. Charitynavigator.org makes this easy; just type in the name of the group and you can get a report on their operations, including how much they spend on programs versus administration and fundraising.

☑ Quick Tip: Giving to Charity for Free

Signing up to become an organ donor, giving blood, giving away used clothes or books, and volunteering for a morning at a local soup kitchen can have at least as much of an impact as running in a charity race or donating $100 once a year. You can also use the opportunity to donate and clean out your closet or bookshelves at the same time. If you have a big enough pile of stuff, some charities are willing to stop by and pick it up, saving you a trip. To find the right group, do a web search for what you have—"used clothes," for example—and your city. When I searched for "donate books" and "Washington, DC," I found Books for America, a nonprofit that collects books for local libraries, schools, and shelters. Within a few days, the group took about sixty books off my hands. Now, someone else can enjoy Malcolm Gladwell's *The Tipping Point* and Zadie Smith's *On Beauty*.

Say you find yourself drawn to Habitat for Humanity International, a nonprofit that builds homes for needy families and is perhaps most famous for organizing groups of college volunteers for spring break trips. If you have fond memories of one of those spring break trips yourself, and you want to reduce homelessness in the world, then you might consider supporting this group. Its Charity Navigator report shows that 85 percent of its budget goes toward programs, which is better than the typical 75 percent, so you know that 85 cents of every dollar you give is going directly toward the nonprofit's mission. (Administrative costs make up about 4 percent of the budget and the rest goes toward fundraising.) You can even see that the chief executive earns just over a quarter of a million dollars a year, which might give you pause about your own career plans but hardly seems exorbitant for the head of such a large organization. The four-star rating also indicates that you can feel reasonably comfortable turning over your hard-earned money (or vacation time) to this group.

Compare that to the American Red Cross, which was downgraded from four stars to two after revenue dropped off and it started spending less on programs. That doesn't mean you shouldn't donate to the Red Cross, which comes to people's aid after emergencies—it just means that you should be aware of some of its recent financial challenges. Charities with one or two stars, such as the Boys Choir of Harlem, which puts two-thirds of its budget toward administrative costs and just one-third toward programs, are probably worth investigating further before making a donation.

BUDGETING FROM THE HEART

So, now that you have your checkbook out, how many zeroes should you include? The answer, of course, depends on your budget. If you're already meeting your savings goals, then you have more leeway to dedicate your surplus funds to charities. Another option is to scale back other spending so you can give more money away. You can also make sure to direct already budgeted money toward altruistic alternatives—for example, you could choose charity events when spending your entertainment dollars and buy gifts for friends from your favorite charitable organization's online store. Only you know the dollar amount you feel comfortable giving, but here's a little peer-to-peer comparison: people with higher education levels tend to have higher giving rates (as well as higher salaries, of course). Nine in ten of those with graduate degrees give to charity, according to the Center on Philanthropy at Indiana University. Their gifts tend to be larger, too. The median annual donation among people with high school diplomas is $700, compared to $1,260 for those with college degrees and $2,055 for those holding graduate degrees.[5]

College graduates donate, on average, 2.4 percent of their annual income. That means our average young professional Kenneth, who is now earning close to $100,000 a year at age thirty-five, would need to donate $2,400 to be average. Since he and Danielle still find their own budget strained by the cost of child care, they give less than that—around $500 a year to a children's charity in Ecuador. To augment that amount, they also asked for donations in lieu of birthday presents this year.

Exercises: Are You a Skilled Giver?

1. Is there a cause that's caught your eye that you'd like to act on? Maybe it's the homeless shelter you pass on your way to work each day or that voting rights organization you keep reading about in the paper. Ask around and see if your friends have any of their own ideas, or if you share any interests in the same causes. Then consider looking into the ways that you could help: Volunteering on a Saturday morning? Spearheading a fundraising drive? Helping the shelter organize its annual walk-a-thon?

2. Check out the young professionals' organizations at local museums. For a small membership fee that goes toward supporting the exhibits, you often receive benefits ranging from private tours for visiting family members to regular cocktail hours and invitations to exhibits before they officially open.

3. If you like the atmosphere and camaraderie of book clubs, then consider forming a giving circle. You just need a group of friends interested in meeting up regularly and pooling money to give to a charity. If your group grows, then you might want to consider filing some paperwork to become an official organization or nonprofit. But to start, you can just meet up with friends, do your research together, and then write checks directly to the charity of your choice.

4. Write down your giving priorities. Even if you give away just $200 a year, don't let it slip away at each request from a coworker or acquaintance running in the annual 10K. Instead, decide which causes are important to you and set aside the amount of money you want to give to them. If

you get requests that don't reflect your goals, then decline them. (Of course, if your best friend is raising money for a cure for leukemia, you might want to consider writing her a check of support regardless of whether that's one of your own passions.)

5. Take a look at the nonfinancial ways you can start giving to charity. Do you give blood? Does your apartment have a closet full of books or clothes that you wouldn't miss? Do you have an afternoon each week (or month) that you could dedicate to an underprivileged little brother or sister, a rain forest preservation campaign, or reading to the blind?

12

NONPROFIT DREAMIN'

For some people, donating money to an organization or volunteering on weekends isn't enough. They want to create institutions that address the problems they see, whether it's genocide halfway around the world, struggling inner cities, or girls who are short-changed in American schools. Starting a nonprofit can be the best way to work on issues everyone else seems to be ignoring, which is one reason almost one hundred nonprofits get started every day.[1] But it can also be a recipe for wasted time and money.

In this chapter, you'll learn the following:

1. Why starting a nonprofit can be a satisfying (and challenging) decision

2. What drives young professionals to start their own organizations

3. When it makes more sense to join up with existing forces instead

STARTING A NONPROFIT

Hamtramck, a city on the northern edge of Detroit, might be best known for its Polish donuts, or paczkis (pronounced "ponshkies"), consumed across the city on Fat Tuesday. Despite its thriving immigrant community of Polish families and more recently arrived Bangladeshis, it suffered from the same recession that beat up much of the rest of the state. Rising foreclosures and rapidly falling property prices meant that, in early 2009, some older, dilapidated houses were selling for less than the cost of a used Chevy. Those prices, and the efforts of some artists to buy and renovate them, caught the eye of ABC's *20/20* producers, who profiled the project.

The show aired on a Friday night in the spring of 2009, and Ian Perrotta, along with his twin, Dan, both twenty-four-year-old seniors at the University of Pittsburgh at the time, happened to be watching. Ian had been noticing the falling property prices in Detroit for a while. When he saw some houses selling for $100, he said to his brother, "It's too bad we don't live in Detroit. We'd know a cool area to get a house." When the *20/20* special confirmed his hunch that Detroit's tough times had also made the city into a land of opportunity, Ian went online and checked out some of the houses for sale on craigslist .org. He saw a couple in Hamtramck listed for $100 to $200. He wanted to check out the houses firsthand, so that night he and Dan got into Ian's black 1997 Dodge Dakota pickup truck and drove the five hours to Detroit. He wanted to see for himself whether Detroit was the right place to build the nonprofit he'd been daydreaming about.

Ian's vision is far grander than flipping old houses in a rundown neighborhood. He wants to revitalize the area by creating something of a social utopia (although he hesitates to call it that). He's repulsed by the materialistic culture epitomized by shows such as MTV's *My Super Sweet Sixteen* and blames the country's financial troubles on rampant consumerism. "People were walking around with $400 purses but wouldn't give $1 to a bum. . . . It disgusted me. Starting this was a way for me to take action and to do something good," he says, his voice speeding up with excitement. His goal, he explains, is not to make money but to renovate the houses and then give them, free of charge, to professionals who in turn pledge their services to the community one day a week. A nurse might open her door to the neighborhood on Mondays; likewise, a dental hygienist, financial planner, paralegal, and social worker would welcome those who needed help, one day a week. "If they didn't have the burden of a mortgage to pay, they would be able to use their skills to help other people in the community," Ian says. He plans to offer the professionals three-year contracts, which stipulate that they can live in the homes in exchange for a day a week of their services. Meanwhile, he'd like to manage the nonprofit while working as a professional firefighter in the town. (He previously served as a volunteer firefighter in college.)

One of his goals is to create the sense of community that he's only experienced through old movies and books. "Now you don't know your neighbors; you're just inside on a computer. This is trying to create more of a communal society, where people help each other out," he says.

When Ian and his brother arrived at one of the listed houses close to dawn on that spring morning, Ian liked what he saw. The 2,700-square-foot brick house was everything he had envisioned it would be. While it was hardly "move-in ready" for the average buyer—it lacked the hookups for running water and electricity, for starters—it was priced to sell and Ian was eager to start working on it. He also didn't mind living in such conditions, which he dubs "colonial living." So he paid the $100 asking price and also purchased five other similarly priced houses nearby for a total initial outlay of $1,400, including fees. (He used money that he had happened to earn from investing in GM stock earlier in the year, which he took as another sign that Detroit was the right place for him.) That brick house now serves as

Ian's home and organization headquarters. While he acknowledges that some might describe the neighborhood as "sketchy," he focuses on the friendliness of his neighbors, who have been welcoming, and curious about his project.

On the surface, Ian might sound like an idealistic, or even naïve, college student. He certainly looks like one; for a meeting with the mayor of Hamtramck, he wore a black T-shirt and jeans. But his vision is hardly a pipe dream. He's making it come true, partly through savvy manipulation of the media and celebrity culture.

As he and his brother were starting up their organization, Dan emailed celebrity blogger Perez Hilton. "Hey Perez, I know you're a busy guy, but you post about good causes once in a while. Here's a good cause, and it would be cool if you could post about it," the email said. Somehow, Perez saw the email and wrote up a post. That day, the Habitat for Hamtramck website received one thousand hits and about the same number of donated dollars.

Then, the brothers took it to the next level: on a newly created website (isstephencolbertacoward.com), they publicly challenged Stephen Colbert to help them raise $350,000 in exchange for having one of the renovated houses named after him. (So far, Colbert has ignored the challenge, a status that Ian says he doesn't expect to change until their nonprofit filings are finalized.)

The Perez Hilton publicity attracted volunteers willing to contribute to the renovation work, as well as the pro bono assistance of a lawyer in Minnesota who offered to help the organization gain official nonprofit status by filing the appropriate paperwork on Ian's behalf. (She has already suggested that Ian change the name of the organization because Habitat for Hamtramck sounds too similar to Habitat for Humanity, which could cause Michigan to deny the application. She has also pointed out some potential problems, such as the challenge of monitoring the services performed by the professionals and what happens if the nonprofit gets sued because someone feels they received bad advice. Ian is now working out those issues.) Within a few months, Ian expects the organization to be a fully functioning nonprofit well on its way to renovating its first house, with possible plans to expand to other cities.

As Ian discovered, starting a nonprofit is similar to launching your own business in many ways. You start with a mission statement and business plan, and the paperwork builds from there. If you're the kind of person who finds keeping up with health insurance forms challenging, then you might want to enlist outside help. (Law firms and other large companies are often willing to take on pro bono projects for a good cause. Some law schools, such as Yale Law School, offer free assistance to groups seeking nonprofit status by connecting the organizations to students doing related coursework.) Some people, like Ian, get their nonprofit off the ground with very low start-up expenses. Aside from the cost of his home purchases, he relied largely on the help of volunteers.

To achieve official nonprofit, or 501(c)(3), status, which makes donations tax-deductible, you need to file the appropriate forms with the IRS and your state, as Ian is doing. That can cost anywhere from $300 to $700, depending on the size of your organization. (The specific requirements for achieving nonprofit status vary by state; you can find more information on your state's website as well as at irs.gov.) Nonprofits must have a charitable, religious, educational, or scientific purpose. It usually takes at least six months to achieve nonprofit status and, of course, not all applications are accepted.

Then, it's time to get the funding you need in order to launch your idea. Fundraising expert Reynold Levy, president of the Lincoln Center for the Performing Arts and author of *Yours for the Asking: An Indispensable Guide to Fundraising and Management*, recommends that you think of fundraising like job hunting: start with your contacts, including former classmates, and build out from there. Social networking sites such as Facebook make it easy to spread the word.

When asked why he doesn't just bypass all that hard work and instead join up with a similar organization like Habitat for Humanity,

Ian's answer sounds similar to that of other twenty-somethings who are used to emphasizing their individuality. "I don't want to be micro-managed by someone. I want to do it my way and don't want to do something by other people's rules," he explains. That line of thinking is not so different from the reasoning of another young nonprofit founder, Lindsay Hyde, although their similarities end there.

Q. Why do so many celebrities form nonprofits? Do they actually make a difference?

A. Celebrities have a vast network of resources at their disposal—not only from their own wealth, but from the collected wealth of their fans and friends. They also often feel passionately about causes related to their own success. The Fugees' Wyclef Jean, a native of Haiti, started the foundation Yéle Haiti to support education and community development in his home country. Michael Phelps started his eponymous foundation to promote the sport of swimming and healthy, active lifestyles for kids with the million-dollar bonus he received after he won his eighth gold medal at the 2008 Beijing Olympics. Other celebrities, such as Ashton Kutcher, help to boost the visibility of existing organizations. Ashton increased awareness around malaria prevention after donating $100,000 to the nonprofit Malaria No More. (After Ashton made his pledge, Larry King and Oprah Winfrey, among others, also donated money to the cause.)

As for whether celebrities make a difference, the answer is yes. Wyclef has already raised millions for programs in Haiti, and Michael Phelps donated $1 million from his foundation to the Boys and Girls Club, where he also works directly with kids. Ashton Kutcher's money bought ten thousand mosquito nets for African families. In addition to money, celebrities have the added advantage of being able to bring publicity to their causes more easily than the rest of us.

Whereas Ian comes across as a youthful, light-haired twenty-five-year-old who would easily blend in with a group of college students, twenty-eight-year-old Lindsay Hyde conveys an authority reminiscent of that of a high school principal. During a recent speech at a leadership meeting for Coca-Cola executives, she urged audience members almost twice her age to pursue their "audacious beliefs," whether that involves getting the whole office to recycle or having a civil conversation with their sixteen-year-old.

While Ian is just starting his nonprofit journey, Lindsay has been working at hers for almost a decade. When she first arrived at Harvard as a freshman, she looked around for mentoring programs where she could work with younger girls. After being raised by a single mom in south Florida as a teen, she has always believed in the power of adult women to serve as role models for their younger counterparts. When she discovered that local mentoring programs weren't accepting undergraduates as volunteers, Lindsay decided to organize her own team of volunteers. "Especially in Boston, with such a huge number of college students, it seemed like a huge workforce not being utilized. . . . I knew we could provide unique value," she says. She rounded up about eight of her fellow freshmen and found two elementary schools interested in working with them. That first year, working from a curriculum that Lindsay had written, the mentors worked with thirty elementary school girls in an afterschool program.

She continued the program throughout college, and when she graduated she received a post-graduate fellowship that let her work on it full-time and officially incorporate into a nonprofit, with the name Strong Women, Strong Girls. She discovered a lot of interest from college students throughout Boston, and she connected those volunteers with elementary schools interested in the after-school program for their third-, fourth-, and fifth-grade girls. She continued to hone the curriculum, which revolves around women's history, self-esteem building, and volunteer projects. Strong Women, Strong Girls has since expanded to Pittsburgh and Miami and connects over one hundred college mentors with more than four hundred girls a year.

Part of the reason Lindsay's nonprofit has expanded so rapidly and successfully is that she spent her first year after college doing a lot of research. "I spent six months sitting down with other people who had started nonprofits and asked them, 'What did you do right? What did you do wrong? What questions do you wish you had asked?'" Lindsay says. "There are plenty of great people willing to share their expertise if you know the right questions to ask." That's one reason she knew that she needed outside help with the accounting side of nonprofit management, which she initially found in the form of a volunteer. Lindsay continues to rely on the expertise of her board of directors, which currently includes an accountant, a pediatrician, and a business consultant, to provide guidance and support.

She also got help with fundraising from a public service organization at her alma mater, which helped her kick off the nonprofit's first year with a budget of $60,000. Today, she pays herself and ten full-time equivalents a salary. The income is enough to allow her to save for retirement and meet other financial goals, but nowhere close to what her peers who went into law or banking earn. This is not surprising, since an analysis by CareerBuilder found nonprofit salaries to be routinely lower than those in the corporate sector. A corporate attorney, for example, earns an average of almost $114,000, while a nonprofit lawyer earns an average of just over $64,000.[2] At the same time, Lindsay's self-employment gives her some measure of job security at a time when unemployment is running close to 10 percent, and closer to 20 percent for her age bracket.

Meanwhile, Lindsay continues to manage the day-to-day challenges of running a nonprofit: she navigates the bureaucracy of school systems, develops relationships with donors, and constantly updates the curriculum so the same girls can participate for consecutive years. She plans to continue expanding Strong Women, Strong Girls and to bring it to more cities. But ultimately, she explains, "as with any nonprofit, the goal is to put yourself out of business—to get to the place where we're not needed anymore because we'll have solved the fundamental problem."

Childhood friends Judd Schneider, Tony MacDonald, and Mike Richton also dream of a world where their services are no longer needed. The Massachusetts-based trio, now in their early thirties, started StopLeukemia.org after each had a firsthand experience with the disease: Judd's father and Tony's friend died from it, and Mike's mother, diagnosed at age fifty, is a survivor. After years of participating in charity events to raise money for research and big organizations such as the Dana-Farber Cancer Institute, they decided to start their own group to focus on helping families. "We came together and said, 'If we put all of our energy and resources into one place, we'll be much more successful,'" says Mike, who works in sales. They also wanted to make sure the majority of the donations—at least 95 percent—were going toward families, instead of toward overhead costs, which sometimes happens at bigger organizations.

In addition to helping people share their own experiences with leukemia on the website and raising awareness of the bone marrow registry, they are also raising money to help cover the expenses that families face during treatment for leukemia, such as hotel stays and gas. By working with hospitals, they distribute the money to families who need the help.

Like Lindsay and Ian, they've come across people willing to lend assistance along the way. The lawyer who helped them achieve 501(c)(3) status worked for a discounted rate, a web designer donated his services, and others made donations to the organization's first raffle and silent auction. For their first event, held at a bar and featuring speeches from Mike's mother and a hospital representative, a band offered to play for no charge. They ended up raising $10,000.

Unlike Lindsay and Ian, Judd, Tony, and Mike maintain full-time jobs outside of their nonprofit work. (Like Mike, Tony works in sales and Judd is a consultant.) "It's a difficult juggling act. We try to have most of the conversations between the three of us in off hours, first thing in the morning or in the evenings or weekends. It's definitely challenging, but it's something we want to do," says Mike. Their financial skills from work have also given them a leg up when it comes to running their organization.

Lindsay and Ian, along with Judd, Tony and Mike, follow in the footsteps of other young nonprofit founders, such as Wendy Kopp. It was Wendy who developed the idea for Teach for America as part of her college thesis and after graduating turned it into the massive program that it is today. Like their predecessors, they are succeeding largely because they seek out (and receive) the help of others. But sometimes, that initial stage of research suggests that it makes more sense to join forces with an existing nonprofit than it does to start your own.

JOIN THE CLUB

In what can sound like the cynicism of age trying to suffocate the idealism of youth, many experienced nonprofit experts urge people to contribute to established organizations instead of creating new ones. In some cases, that's good advice. "Fundamentally, there are too many nonprofit organizations in the United States. Somebody starting his or her own nonprofit ought to ask, 'Am I likely to have the most impact by starting my own organization, or by contributing my services and money to an existing organization?'" suggests Paul Brest, coauthor of *Money Well Spent*.

But many young professionals, who have been brought up in the era of personalized Facebook pages, individualized iTunes playlists, and customized college courses, don't want to toe an existing organization's line. They also have fresh ideas and new approaches to old problems that don't fit into existing models. According to figures from the Urban Institute's National Center for Charitable Statistics, the number of nonprofits has grown 30 percent over the last decade, which averages out to about one hundred new nonprofits each day.[3]

But that doesn't mean creating a nonprofit is an easy thing to do. "There are a number of people approaching us who are fueled by the myth of nonprofits," says Tim Delaney, chief executive of the National Council of Nonprofits, who teaches classes on the subject. First-timers often think it will be a fun and straightforward way of fulfilling a dream, and Delaney says he has to set them straight. "I discovered the best service I could provide as a teacher was to spend the first third of class explaining why they should not create a new nonprofit," he explains, citing headaches such as paperwork, liabilities, and worrying about keeping up with payroll demands. "If you are truly motivated by a passion to serve, it might be better to find an existing nonprofit where you can channel that positive energy without having to worry about the nuances of the state and federal forms that go into forming a nonprofit," he adds. If other organizations with similar goals already exist, then it will also be difficult to continually raise enough money to support your own efforts (after exhausting the generosity of your friends and family members).

Of course, working with an existing nonprofit isn't always as straightforward as it sounds, either. When my sister, Christina Palmer, now a fourth-year medical student at the University of Pennsylvania, traveled to Bangalore, India, several years ago to volunteer in a nonprofit-run health clinic, she arrived to find that the group did not have the clinic that they had described to her. She found herself alone in India with no project. "At that point I started networking like crazy, visiting different nonprofits, and talking with friends of friends," she says. She soon discovered Operation Shanti, a nonprofit that works with homeless women and children on the streets of Mysore, a town a couple hours southwest of Bangalore. Christina quickly packed up her bags and moved there.

When she arrived, she found just what she was looking for. With the support of a well-run nonprofit behind her, she went into the streets every day and got to know a group of impoverished women and children. She helped enroll the children in school and the women to find jobs and homes. Many of them had HIV, TB, and other health issues, so she helped bring them to doctors' appointments and taught them about their medications. "The women and children on the streets immediately took me in, shared their life, gave me chai, and put jasmine flowers in my hair. One girl, Asha, had left school to live on the streets and care for her mother who was dying of AIDS. They slept next to each other on old yoga mats on the pavement. We loaned Asha money to start up a flower business. She would wake up early and stay up late working, bringing back food and money to her mother," says Christina, adding that she not only felt like she was helping this group of women and children but also got to "eat with them, laugh with them, and pray with them."

Although Christina had to use some of her savings to pay for this trip, she says it gave her insight and direction into what she wanted out of her medical career, so it was well worth the effort. She continues to travel to other countries and work in public health; she recently returned from working in an AIDS clinic in Botswana.

Kenneth and Danielle, the composite young professionals representing many of us, wrestled with the question of how best to give back. They knew they wanted to use their resources—including their money, time, and skills—to help eradicate poverty in Ecuador. After giving to a children's charity for a couple of years, they came to the conclusion that they could best contribute by helping families take out small loans to get their businesses off the ground. That way, they would be helping the families establish a method of supporting themselves into the future. Kenneth's business background also drew him to the microlending world; he believed larger economic growth could be fueled by the entrepreneurial spirit.

As they started their research, Kenneth and Danielle came across kiva.org, a web-based nonprofit that connects investors to entrepreneurs around the world. After providing a loan (usually between $25 and $500) to one of the entrepreneurs profiled on the site, donors can keep track online of how they are doing. Once the loan is repaid, donors can opt to invest in someone else's business. Kiva lists dozens of entrepreneurs in retail, construction, and other businesses throughout South America. Kenneth and Danielle sat down at their computer with their daughter Sophia, who was now old enough to contribute to the decision about where to invest the $500 they had set aside for this purpose. Sophia liked the pink colors of the children's clothes from the store in Quito that her parents pointed out to her. She wanted to help that store owner expand her business. Her parents agreed. So together, they made the donation. After clicking the "submit" button, they talked about planning a visit on their next family vacation, and perhaps buying Sophia a new pink outfit at the store they had helped to grow.

For Kenneth, that was just the beginning of what would eventually become a second career for him. On the family's subsequent visit to Ecuador, he realized that many of the small businesses were hungry for more information and advice on how to best grow and expand. So he started a mentoring program that matches up small-business owners in Ecuador with those in small towns across the United States. Through a Facebook-like social networking program, the business owners ask each other questions, get advice, and share frustrations. Soon, Kenneth began getting requests from business owners in other countries who were looking for the same kind of answers. As his mentoring network took off, he arranged a new schedule with his consulting job to allow him to spend two days a week working on it. He works from home on those days, which means he's there when Sophia gets home from school. As he develops new partnerships and corporate sponsorships, he imagines eventually working full-time for his organization. Now that he and Danielle are expecting Sophia's new baby brother, he's grateful for the schedule change and the fact that he has found more satisfying work, even though he has had to sacrifice some of his salary. But for Kenneth and Danielle, that was a price they were willing to pay.

Exercises: Is There a Nonprofit in Your Future?

1. Consider the unmet needs in your community. Who needs help that they're not getting?

2. Over the course of the next month or so, pay attention to the global issues in the news that most interest you. Is there an area that intrigues you so much that you'd like to get involved?

3. Write down your vision for a potential nonprofit in a few sentences. Search the Web to see if anything similar already exists. If it does, consider volunteering for the organization. If it doesn't, explore dipping your toes into nonprofit work by organizing a volunteer project.

4. If you decide to go ahead and form your own nonprofit, first make a list of all the resources at your disposal. Whom could you ask for advice? Who has done something similar? What friends or other groups in your network might be willing to support you? Websites such as foundationcenter.org, socialedge.org, and oceangrand.org can provide guidance.

Epilogue: Redefining Rich

As I worked on this book over the course of a year or so, many of the people in it experienced major changes. They launched businesses, found new jobs, moved to different cities, and had kids. Along with their lifestyles, their financial situations shifted too.

Kimberly Wilson, the yoga teacher and entrepreneur we met in chapter 1, opened her new studio and it quickly filled up with students, despite the ongoing recession. As they enter, visitors are greeted with the relaxing scent of lavender and a display of Kimberly's brightly colored line of wraps and dresses, along with a bookshelf full of self-improvement titles and a tray of tea and cookies. The studio incorporates a slew of eco-friendly features: natural light floods through huge skylights in the practice rooms and the bathrooms offer low-flush options. The floors are made out of recycled wood and renewable resources such as bamboo and cork. Heavy insulation reduces the need for air-conditioning and heating. Students are offered a water fountain instead of plastic bottles of water. Through the nonprofit Trees for the Future, the studio also plants a tree for every class pass and massage that's purchased. Although the building costs ended up being higher than anticipated and Kimberly had to tap additional lines of credit in order to finish the project, she says the investment is paying off.

As for her other big goal, buying a cabin for weekend getaways in West Virginia, her boyfriend ended up making the purchase, which lets the couple escape from the city on as many weekends as they can. "It's so nice to have that space, and to look out on trees instead of concrete," says Kimberly.

After the economy slowed down, Kimberly dialed back some of her daily spending. "I became really mindful of not indulging in runs to Target, or Whole Foods. It's amazing how you can go out and spend $100. I didn't cut out manicures and pedicures, but I cut out the miscellaneous things—like candles, or shoes," she says. She decided to add a couple weeks in between trips to the hair salon, too. "I still get in my indulgences, but in smaller doses, and with more time in between them," she says, adding that those minor changes add up to significant savings.

Tim Bradley and Anne Morrison Bradley, the couple going into business for themselves, also contended with the challenges of starting up amid a recession. They officially launched their pet decor site, The Premium Pet, in August 2009. Unexpected website glitches, time-consuming data entry for each product, and last-minute updates meant putting in long hours after getting home from their full-time jobs, and eating a lot of microwaveable meals. During the first two weeks, they received an order from a customer in the United Kingdom for a corner dog bed. But because he lived overseas, the shipping through UPS would have cost $500, making it prohibitively expensive. Tim and Anne had to ask the customer to pay an additional shipping charge so they could have the item shipped to their home and then mail it themselves from the post office. This turned out to be a cheaper method, although it was more labor intensive for Tim and Anne.

Partly because of the continuing recession, Tim and Anne are careful to match the prices of their competitors on all their merchandise, and they're putting off spending money on advertising until their site is fully populated with dozens of products in each category. "We're pretty cautious about expenditures at this point," says Anne.

"The little things added up to a lot more time than we anticipated. We were concentrating so much on product entry that we didn't realize how much time it would take for other parts of the site," such as writing the "about us" page or the "customer care" section, Anne explains. Those extra hours took a toll on their other obligations. "The house is getting dirtier—we come home and start working," says Tim. The couple has also cut back on social activities and sleep as they try to get the site off the ground. "It's enjoyable when we're doing it, but when we're exhausted and have to get up to go to work in the morning, it's hard," says Anne.

"I thought we'd be farther along right now. Both of us thought that once the site was launched that it would be a great success. While it is, we both understand the mountain of work that's still ahead, and we've only begun to chip away at it. We're nowhere near the place we'd like to be, where we can sit back and watch the sales roll in," says Tim. Anne adds that, unlike with companies that have been in the market for a while, any sale is still exciting. "We have no expectations of income, so anything better than zero is a good thing." By the end of the first month, The Premium Pet had already made its first $1,000 of sales revenue.

Mitch Wrosch, the twenty-nine-year-old attorney from chapter 3 who plans to pay off his student loan debt in full as soon as he is able to, discovered that he was eligible for the income-based repayment plan that began in 2009, which means that for his lower-interest federal loans his monthly payments max out at 15 percent of his income. Because he earned a low salary as a law clerk and then no salary while studying in Israel, that new program will reduce his payments, at least temporarily. He recently accepted a job doing constitutional litigation in Los Angeles, which means his income, along with his payments, will likely go up. "My financial goals now are to continue maintaining a zero balance on my credit cards and to pay the absolute minimum on my federal loans in order to pay off my $30,000 in private loans more quickly," he says.

Veronica Neilan, the health counseling graduate student who needed an emergency root canal, became increasingly frugal as she graduated amid the recession and high unemployment rates. After applying for dozens of jobs, she received only one interview request, and it was for a job that required only a high school degree. "Three years ago, when I was looking for a job as an undergrad with a bachelor's in psychology, I got more people calling me for interviews than I do now," she says. She's been sending her resume and cover letter to almost every social service agency in the area and has received mostly form letter rejections in return.

She decided to move from Brooklyn to her mother's house in New Hampshire while she continues job hunting. "It stresses me out a lot," she says, especially since she has $113,000 in student loans to pay back. "I can ride out the grace period, but I'd feel better if I knew I was going to have a job." The experience has taught her to be more wary of taking on debt. "I don't want to be the person who buys a house they can't afford," she says.

Meanwhile, Nicole Mladic, the public relations executive we met in chapter 5, continues on her savings trajectory, and her net worth has almost reached the $100,000 mark. She plans to use some of those funds to buy a house or condo. She decided to leave her job at a public relations firm, where she had climbed the ladder for eight years, to head up communications for Northwestern University's Feinberg School of Medicine, partly for the extra job stability. "My biggest issue now is that I'm in such good financial shape that I have to work really hard not to spend frivolously. It takes discipline," Nicole says. To deal with that, she's turning to online programs that track spending.

Keith and Katy Hewson, the couple in Houston who lived with Katy's parents, Cindy and Gary Smith, first in the Smiths' townhouse and then in the Hewsons' newly purchased home, are now preparing for another addition to the household: their first child. After considering whether it was time to start living on their own, they decided the benefits continued to outweigh any cons, so they invited Katy's parents to continue living with them. The soon-to-be grandparents are moving from the top floor into the downstairs bedroom, which still has its own bathroom and patio, to give the young family more space upstairs. Keith maintains his extensive travel schedule for his job as a pilot, which makes the Smiths' live-in assistance even more valuable. The savings generated from the arrangement continue to fund international trips for both couples: before the baby's arrival, the Smiths are going on a cruise to Rome and the Greek isles and Keith and Katy are traveling to Amsterdam.

After welcoming their baby daughter into their family, Dan and Kellie Mercurio decided to continue their separate banking system, and they created a custodial savings account for their daughter as well. That's where any gift money goes. Since Kellie became a stay-at-home mom, they divide Dan's paycheck into the various accounts for household expenses and their individual expenses. The switch to a single income, says Dan, "isn't changing the way we use the accounts, it just tightens our budget."

Lawyer and mom Lindsay Kelly experienced a tough work year during her daughter's first year. She was away from home for almost a month at an intense trial and worked long hours at the office in the months leading up to it. Now, partly because of her increased experience and tenure at the firm, she's been able to work on smaller cases that she runs herself, which means she's more in control of the pace of her work. Because she's not working as part of a large team, it's easier for her to work from home two to three days a week. "It has been relaxing for me and a real benefit for the kids," she says. She and her husband, George, bought a house in Georgetown and switched from a full-time nanny to about six college-age babysitters who rotate days, which gives Lindsay more flexibility to send them home early or change their hours at the last minute. "It's administratively more complicated, because I generally need to hire at least one new person each semester, including summers, but I'm very happy with this arrangement," she says.

Jennifer Rescigno, the recruiter in her late thirties who chose to delay having kids until she felt she could afford them, has yet to find a job with maternity benefits, which means she and her husband are still waiting to start a family.

Habitat for Hamtramck founder Ian Perrotta started renovating his first house in the ailing Detroit neighborhood. The yard, kitchen, bathroom, and rest of the house were filled with garbage, including old couches, weights, and sewage. That last item meant Ian had to set up a ventilation system with an industrial fan to keep the air safe while he and his brother worked. With an eye on the potential publicity that would come from being sued, Ian has also decided to keep the organization's original name. "One of the best possible things that could happen to us would be for Habitat for Humanity to sue for trademark infringement. The exposure it could give us would be incredible and the 'court of public opinion' would look favorably on us and see them as the bad guys," says Ian. He continues to move forward with his nonprofit application. And he's still waiting to hear back from Stephen Colbert.

As for me, as our baby's due date approached, we called off our house search. We decided we'd rather keep our money in the bank to help us through a period that was sure to be filled with unexpected costs as we figured out how to be parents. Though the decision to fit our family of three into our small apartment might not have boasted of material wealth, knowing we were living within our means was worth much more to us. We were hardly alone in feeling that way. The 2009 Pew Economic Mobility Project found that, when it comes to defining the American dream, respondents ranked being financially secure ahead of owning a house, earning enough income to afford luxuries, and becoming rich.[1]

Our tight quarters didn't last forever. When our daughter was three months old, we bought a house that we love—and could afford, thanks in part to the fact that we had paid a relatively low rent for so long. Now, we continue to monitor our budget closely, as we incorporate child-care costs, a mortgage, and other baby-related expenses (who knew diapers cost so much?) into our lives.

Our generation might have grown up in an era of relative opulence, but as I make use of a closet full of second-hand baby clothes and a hand-me-down crib, I can't help but feel lucky that we had the chance to learn some of that old-school frugality. Perhaps the economy will be booming again by the time our daughter is old enough to notice the difference; maybe to her our habits will seem as out of date as the Great Depression is to us. Or maybe her generation, having been born into a post-recession world, will continue to embrace sustainability and thriftiness because it seems like the better way to live, even after it's no longer financially necessary.

Endnotes

Introduction

1. Alan Corey, *A Million Bucks by 30: How to Overcome a Crap Job, Stingy Parents, and a Useless Degree to Become a Millionaire Before (or After) Turning Thirty* (New York: Ballantine Books, 2007).

2. Anya Kamenetz, *Generation Debt: Why Now Is a Terrible Time to Be Young* (New York: Riverhead Books, 2005); Carmen Wong Ulrich, *Generation Debt: Take Control of Your Money—A How-To Guide* (New York: Business Plus, 2006).

3. Kara McGuire, "It's Payback Time: Reality Hits College Grads: How to Pay Off Overwhelming Student Loans?" *Minneapolis Star Tribune*, April 28, 2009.

4. "Staying Afloat," *Today*, NBC, June 18, 2008.

5. "Money for Breakfast," Fox Business Network, June 2, 2009.

6. American Council on Education Center for Policy Analysis, "Federal Student Loan Debt: 1993 to 2004," www.acenet.edu.

7. The College Board, "Trends in Student Aid 2009," http://www.trends-college-board.com/student_aid/4_1_loans_h.html?expandable=0.

8. José Garcia, "Borrowing to Make Ends Meet: The Rapid Growth of Credit Card Debt in America," Demos, 2007, 9.

9. National Center for Education Statistics, http://nces.ed.gov.

10. Terry Fitzgerald, "Has Middle America Stagnated?" Federal Reserve Bank of Minneapolis, 2007.

11. *Student Monitor*, www.studentmonitor.com, data emailed to author.

12. José Garcia, Demos analysis of the Survey of Consumer Finances emailed to author.

13. Economic Mobility Project, http://www.economicmobility.org.

Chapter I

1. Gulden Ulkumen, Manoj Thomas, and Vicki Morwitz, "Will I Spend More in 12 Months or a Year? The Effect of Ease of Estimate and Confidence on Budget Estimates," *Journal of Consumer Research* 35 (August 2008).

2. Bureau of Labor Statistics, www.bls.gov/cex/2007/Standard/income.pdf.

3. Bureau of Economic Analysis, http://www.bea.gov/BRIEFRM/SAVING.HTM.

4. Ran Kivetz, Oleg Urminsky, and Yuhuang Zheng, "The Goal-Gradient Hypothesis Resurrected: Purchase Acceleration, Illusionary Goal Progress, and Customer Retention," *Journal of Marketing Research* 43, no. 1 (February 2006): 39–50.

5. José Garcia, "Index Credit Cards," Demos analysis of the Survey of Consumer Finances, emailed to author, www.indexcreditcards.com/creditcardmonitor.

6. Michael I. Norton and Leonard Lee, "The 'Fees → Savings' Link, or Purchasing Fifty Pounds of Pasta" (HBS Working Paper Number: 08-029, November 2007).

7. Eric R. Spangenberg, David E. Sprott, Bianca Grohmann, and Daniel L. Tracy, "Gender-congruent ambient scent influences on approach and avoidance behaviors in a retail store," *Journal of Business Research* 59, 12 (November 2006): 1281–87.

8. Kimberly Palmer, "The Games Companies Play," *US News & World Report*, August 1, 2007.

9. Kimberly Palmer, "Why Shoppers Love to Hate Rebates," *US News & World Report*, January 18, 2008.

10. "Rebates: Get What You Deserve," *Consumer Reports*, September 2009, 7.

11. Bob Sullivan, *Gotcha Capitalism: How Hidden Fees Rip You Off Every Day— And What You Can Do About It* (New York: Ballantine, 2007), 291.

Chapter 2

1. In his book *Multiple Streams of Income*, Robert G. Allen describes how to create different sources of cash by focusing on real estate and stock market investments. While similar in concept, the kind of multistreaming described in this chapter focuses on more active forms of earning money.

2. Bureau of Labor Statistics, www.bls.gov/nls/nlsy79r19.pdf.

3. Darren Rowse, "How Much Money Do Bloggers Make Blogging?" January 2, 2009, http://www.problogger.net/archives/2009/01/02/how-much-money-do-bloggers-make-blogging/.

4. Bureau of Labor Statistics, courtesy of BLS economist Steven Hipple, data emailed to author.

5. U.S. Census Bureau, www.census.gov/hhes/www/macro/032008/perinc/new07_001.htm.

6. "Women Don't Ask," http://www.womendontask.com/stats.html.

7. Kimberly Palmer, "Single Women Don't Save Enough for Retirement," September 19, 2008, www.usnews.com.

8. Kimberly Palmer, "In a Recession, Hiring Celebrity-Style Coaching Pays," March 3, 2009, www.usnews.com.

Chapter 3

1. José Garcia, Demos analysis of the Survey of Consumer Finances emailed to author.

2. These costs are approximations, since the principal is constantly being reduced, which means the interest payments go down over time.

3. "Trends in Student Aid 2009," College Board, http://www.trends-college-board.com/student_aid/4_1_loans_h.html?expandable=0.

4. More details available at http://studentaid.ed.gov.

5. Kimberly Palmer, "Exposing Lenders' Ties to Schools," *US News & World Report*, September 7, 2007.

6. José Garcia, Demos analysis of the Survey of Consumer Finances emailed to author.

7. "Index Credit Cards," www.indexcreditcards.com/creditcardmonitor.

8. AARP Financial. Note: Survey included adults between the ages of 40 and 79.

9. Kimberly Palmer, "Survey: Many Americans Unprepared for Crises," March 31, 2009, www.usnews.com.

Chapter 4

1. Kimberly Palmer, "Gen Y: Investing Is Fun, Not Scary," October 13, 2009, www.usnews.com.

2. Jeff Dominitz, Angela A. Hung, and Joanne K. Yoong, "How Do Mutual Fund Fees Affect Investor Choices?" RAND, 2008.

3. Paola Sapienza, Luigi Zingales, and Dario Maestripieri, "Gender Differences in Financial Risk Aversion and Career Choices Are Affected by Testosterone" (proceedings of the National Academy of Sciences, August 24, 2009).

4. Analysis by Ibbotson Associates, a subsidiary of Morningstar. Note: Returns do not include inflation, which averages 3 percent a year since 1926.

5. "Lost Decade," *Economist*, March 13, 2009, www.economist.com; E. S. Browning, "Stocks Tarnished by 'Lost Decade,'" *Wall Street Journal*, March 26, 2008.

6. Kimberly Palmer, "Maria Bartiromo: Market Movers 2009," *US News & World Report*, March 2009.

7. Kimberly Palmer, "Why You're Making Dumb 401(k) Choices," March 24, 2009, www.usnews.com.

Chapter 5

1. Social Security Administration, 2009 OASDI Trustees Report, www.ssa.gov/OACT/TR/2009/II_highlights.html#76460.

2. "The Maximum Social Security Retirement Benefit," questions about Social Security on www.ssa.gov, http://www.ssa.gov/includes/topiclist.htm.

3. Alicia H. Munnell, Alex Golub-Sass, Richard W. Kopckc, and Anthony Webb, "What Does It Cost to Guarantee Returns?" Center for Retirement Research at Boston College, February 2009.

4. Kimberly Palmer, "Survey: Retirement Is for New Beginnings," August 5, 2008, www.usnews.com.

5. Retirement Shortfall Calculator, www.bankrate.com/calculators/retirement/calculate-retirement-income-money.aspx

6. Kimberly Palmer, "Using Online Retirement Calculators," October 2, 2008, www.usnews.com.

7. Employee Benefit Research Institute, "Average Worker Contribution Rates to 401(k)-Type Plans," March 19, 2009.

8. Committee on Education and Labor, U.S. House of Representatives, "Strengthening Worker Retirement Security," testimony of John C. Bogle, February 24, 2009.

9. Emily Brandon, "Survey: One in Five Companies Have Now Reduced 401(k) Matches," April 23, 2009, www.usnews.com.

10. Michael D. Hurd and Susann Rohwedder, "The Adequacy of Economic Resources in Retirement" (working paper, University Michigan Retirement Research Center, 2008-184, September 2008).

11. Committee on Education and Labor, U.S. House of Representatives, "Strengthening Worker Retirement Security," testimony of John C. Bogle, February 24, 2009.

12. Ibid.

13. Kimberly Palmer, "Moving Money Among Market Volatility," October 23, 2008, www.usnews.com.

14. Kimberly Palmer, "Single Women Don't Save Enough for Retirement," September 19, 2008, www.usnews.com.

15. Kimberly Palmer, "'Active Savers' Start Early and Often," May 19, 2009, www.usnews.com.

Chapter 6

1. Lynne Adler, "More Generations Living Under the Same Roof," Reuters, February 22, 2010.

2. Katherine Newman and Sofya Aptekar, "Sticking Around: Delayed Departure from the Parental Nest in Western Europe," Network on Transitions to Adulthood, May 2006.

3. Pew Research Center, "The Return of the Multi-Generational Family Household," March 18, 2010, http://pewsocialtrends.org/assets/pdf/752-multi-generational-families.pdf.

4. Kimberly Palmer, "Tips for When Relatives Ask for Loans," November 20, 2008, www.usnews.com.

5. Kimberly Palmer, "Survey: Retirement Is for New Beginnings," August 5, 2008, www.usnews.com.

6. Kimberly Palmer, "The New Parent Trap," *US News & World Report*, December 12, 2007.

7. Network on Transitions to Adulthood, www.transad.pop.upenn.edu/trends/index.html.

8. Kimberly Palmer, "The New Parent Trap," *US News & World Report*, December 12, 2007.

9. Network on Transitions to Adulthood, www.transad.pop.upenn.edu/trends/facts_wa.htm.

10. Network on Transitions to Adulthood, www.transad.pop.upenn.edu/trends/index.html.

11. Kimberly Palmer, "The New Parent Trap," *US News & World Report*, December 12, 2007.

Chapter 7

1. Kirk Warren Brown and Tim Kasser, "Are Psychological and Ecological Well-Being Compatible? The Roles of Values, Mindfulness, and Lifestyle," *Social Indicators Research* 74 (2005): 349–68.

2. John Zogby, *The Way We'll Be: The Zogby Report on the Transformation of the American Dream* (New York: Random House, 2008), 124.

3. Kimberly Palmer, "Why You Can Afford to Eat at Home," February 29, 2008, www.usnews.com.

4. "Exactly How Much Housework Does a Husband Create?" University of Michigan News Service, www.ns.umich.edu/htdocs/releases/story.php?id=6452.

5. Bureau of Labor Statistics, www.bls.gov/cex/2007/Standard/income.pdf.

Chapter 8

1. "Study: Marriage Builds Wealth and Divorce Destroys It," *USA Today*, January 18, 2006.

2. Raddon Financial Group, data emailed to author.

3. Bureau of Labor Statistics "Wives Who Earn More Than Their Husbands," 1987 2005, (*1988–2006 Annual Social and Economic Supplements*, Current Population Survey, Table 25), http://www.bls.gov/opub/ted/2007/nov/wk4/art05.htm.

4. Kimberly Palmer, "Why Renters Insurance Is Worth Its (Low) Cost," September 2, 2009, www.usnews.com.

5. Grace W. Bucchianeri, "The American Dream or the American Delusion? The Private and External Benefits of Homeownership," February 2009, http://real.wharton.upenn.edu/~wongg/research/The%20American%20Dream.pdf.

6. Federal Housing Finance Agency, http://www.fhfa.gov/Default.aspx?Page=14.

7. "How Much House Can You Afford?" CNNMoney.com, http://cgi.money.cnn.com/tools/houseafford/houseafford.html.

Chapter 9

1. U.S. Department of Agriculture, "Expenditures on Children by Families, 2008," http://www.cnpp.usda.gov/Publications/CRC/crc2008.pdf, p. iii, 9.

2. Bureau of Labor Statistics, courtesy of BLS economist Steven Hipple.

3. Kimberly Palmer, "The New Mommy Track," *US News & World Report*, August 26, 2007.

4. Ibid.

5. U.S. Census Bureau, www.census.gov/Press-Release/www/releases/archives/facts_for_features_special_editions/013535.html; www.census.gov/Press-Release/www/releases/archives/facts_for_features_special_editions/013412.html.

6. U.S. Census Bureau, www.census.gov/Press-Release/www/releases/archives/families_households/009842.html.

7. Pamela Paul, *Parenting, Inc.* (New York: Henry Holt, 2008), 7.

8. Kimberly Palmer, "Financial Questions Couples Should Ask," *US News & World Report*, May 8, 2008.

Chapter 10

1. U.S. Department of Energy, www.energystar.gov/index.cfm?c=cfls.pr_cfls.

2. "Put an End to Junk Mail," Greenversatic: The Office Blog of the Environmental Protection Agency, February 26, 2009, http://blog.epa.gov/blog/2009/02/26/put-an-end-to-junk-mail/.

3. The Hartman Group, "Organic 2006: Consumer Attitudes and Behavior, Five Years Later & Into the Future," 1.

4. Charles Benbrook et al., "New Evidence Confirms the Nutritional Superiority of Plant-Based Organic Foods," *State of Science Review*, March 2008. http://www.organic-center.org/science.nutri.php?action=view&report_id=126.

5. The Organic Center, www.organic-center.org/kit/TheOrganicCenter_MediaKit_NPEE08.pdf.

6. Gidon Eshel and Pamela Martin, "Diet, Energy and Global Warming," *Earth Interactions* 10 (2006).

7. Lyndsey Layton, "No BPA for Baby Bottles in U.S.," *Washington Post*, March 6, 2009.

8. "Green Living—US," Mintel International Group Ltd. (January 1, 2009).

9. TerraChoice Environmental Marketing, "The Seven Sins of Greenwashing," April 2009, http://sinsofgreenwashing.org/?dl_id=2.

10. Social Investment Forum, www.socialinvest.org/resources/sriguide/srifacts.cfm.

11. *The Kojo Nnamdi Show*, NPR, April 22, 2009, http://wamu.org/programs/kn/09/04/22.php.

Chapter 11

1. Giving Circles Network, www.givingcircles.org.

2. Mya Frazier, "Costly Red Campaign Reaps Meager $18 Million," *Advertising Age*, March 5, 2007, http://adage.com/article?article_id=115287.

3. Government Accountability Office, "Baby Boom Generation," (GAO-06-718, July 2006), 8.

4. Nicholas D. Kristof, "Bill Gates's Next Big Thing," *New York Times*, January 24, 2009.

5. The Center on Philanthropy at Indiana University, courtesy Adriene Davis.

Chapter 12

1. Urban Institute's National Center for Charitable Statistics, http://www.urban.org/center/cnp/index.cfm.

2. Rachel Zupek, "Maximizing a Nonprofit Salary," www.cnn.com, May 16, 2007, http://www.cnn.com/2007/US/Careers/05/16/cb.profit/index.html.

3. Urban Institute's National Center for Charitable Statistics, http://www.urban.org/center/cnp/index.cfm.

Epilogue

1. Economic Mobility Project, http://www.economicmobility.org/poll2009.

About the Author

KIMBERLY PALMER, an award-winning journalist, is the Alpha Consumer columnist and blogger at *US News & World Report*, where she writes about personal finance and consumer trends. She has appeared on NBC's *Today*, CNBC, CNN, and local television and radio shows across the country. She has also written for the *Washington Post*, the *Wall Street Journal*, and the *Asahi Shimbun/ International Herald Tribune* in Tokyo as a Henry Luce scholar. She holds a master's degree in public policy from the University of Chicago and a bachelor's degree in history from Amherst College. Kimberly lives with her husband and daughter in the Washington, DC, area. You can visit her online at www.bykimberlypalmer.com.

Index